WILLIAM G. JOHNSSON

GLIMPSES of GRACE

SCENES FROM MY JOURNEY

REVIEW AND HERALD® PUBLISHING ASSOCIATION
HAGERSTOWN, MD 21740

The author assumes full responsibility for the accuracy of all facts and quotations as cited in this book.

Texts credited to Message are from *The Message*. Copyright © 1993, 1994, 1995, 1996. Used by permission of NavPress Publishing Group.

Texts credited to NIV are from the *Holy Bible, New International Version*. Copyright © 1973, 1978, 1984, International Bible Society. Used by permission of Zondervan Bible Publishers.

Bible texts credited to RSV are from the Revised Standard Version of the Bible, copyright © 1946, 1952, 1971, by the Division of Christian Education of the National Council of Churches of Christ in the U.S.A. Used by permission.

This book was
Edited by Richard W. Coffen
Copyedited by Delma Miller and James Cavil
Designed by Toya Koch
Cover design by Bill Tymeson
Typeset: 10/15 Bookman Light

PRINTED IN U.S.A.

05   04   03   02   01   5   4   3   2   1

R&H Cataloging Service
Johnsson, William George, 1934-
        Glimpses of grace—scenes from my journey.

1. Grace (Theology).   I. Title

                234.1

ISBN 0-8280-1518-X

Dedication

For Reneé,

who brought so much joy to the Johnsson tribe

and whose life of irrepressible generosity and
thoughtfulness is itself

a glimpse of grace.

Contents

Preface

I had a fire in my belly to write a book about grace, so I dredged around for a title, composed an outline, and wrote several chapters.

Then I tore up the manuscript.

The book was all right—and all wrong.

It had solid, biblical material and sound reasoning. It developed logically. But it didn't glow, let alone blaze. The fire hadn't gotten out of my belly and onto the pages.

It was a book *about* grace instead of a book *of* grace. Like so much Christian writing today, it had the earmarks of an observer instead of a participant.

Of all topics, a book about grace ought to be an "inside" work. When grace has touched and changed and blessed my life so much, how can I deal with it as though it's another editorial or another theological essay?

So you'll find this new manuscript intensely personal. Deliberately, intentionally I have shared stories rather than biblical studies. Most of them come directly from my own life; the rest from reading or contacts with people who breathe in the atmosphere of grace.

Grace is so wonderful that it's best expressed by singing. That's why heaven is an endless song.

On this earth, if you're like me and can't sing like the angels, maybe we best simply tell *our* story—which is really *His* story of amazing grace.

That's what I now have tried to do—sketch scenes from my journey.

The fire is out of my belly.

Chapter One

Glimpses of Grace

I DIDN'T DISCOVER GRACE. It was there all along, and I simply became aware of it.

Like the nose on my face, grace was so close to me that I looked right past it. But once I caught a glimpse, I kept coming back for another look.

Try as hard as you may, unaided you never see your nose. You can close your right eye and get a fuzzy outline of the left side, or shut your left eye and see part of the blurry right side. But you never see the whole thing.

Just like grace. It's so big and so wonderful that you can never see it all. Just glimpses. But those glimpses keep you wanting to see more.

I grew up in Australia. The Great South Land, with its vast open spaces, brooding outback, and magnificent beaches, conjures up superlatives, but "graceful" isn't one of them. The land is harsh, and so is the national character. Aussies are practical, direct, blunt to the point of rudeness, wary of education, and suspicious of those who affect diplomacies and delicacies of speech.

My father, Joel Johnsson, was born in Sweden. He became a seaman in his early teens and sailed the world. When he eventually left his ship in the port of

Adelaide in southern Australia, the only English he knew consisted of cusswords.

But he found the Lord and the Seventh-day Adventist Church in Adelaide. This big strapping Swede became a gentle, pious follower of Jesus who started every day by reading the Bible and taking a cold shower, who taught a Sabbath school class until he was 80, and who served his church as an elder and lay preacher.

From my dad I learned rectitude and strict adherence to principle. From my mother I caught my first glimpse of grace.

Edith was a little woman, a good nine or 10 inches shorter than her husband, but she possessed a feisty spirit and a heart of love. She bore Joel 10 children, one of whom died at birth. I was born last.

When I think of my mother, it's difficult to picture her not working. Cooking, washing, ironing, darning, gardening—she had boundless energy. Her life was a ceaseless giving of herself as she found a way to make ends meet. We were a large family, but we never lacked plenty to eat and never lacked demonstrations of love. Dad found it hard to bring himself to express praise for a good report card, but Mother never held herself back.

Long before I heard of unconditional love, I experienced it. Long before I heard of grace, my mother gave me a glimpse of it.

Many years later I learned that my coming into the world was touched by grace even before I appeared.

Dad was big and strong, hardworking and godly. He worked with his hands for an Adventist builder contractor named Walter Weir. Years later, long after Dad had quit work, I would meet people who'd tell me my dad was the best and most honest worker they'd ever known.

The eighth surviving Johnsson child, Margaret, was born in 1930. By then the family fortunes had taken a nosedive: The stock market crash of 1929 sent shock waves around the world, and the Australian economy slumped along with America's. As always in a depression, the building industry took the first and hardest hit. Dad was laid off, and the Johnsson children went from boys and girls with plenty of toys and birthday parties to the children of poor parents.

We lived in an old house by the river. Out back was a double-sized lot, big enough to keep a cow. It also was dotted with olive and almond trees. We grew our own vegetables and harvested the olives and almonds, which we sold to bring in a little money.

Four years after Margaret, yet another child joined the family. I must have been a shock to everyone—especially to Mother who, at age 42, thought her baby-tending days were past. Already well-meaning relatives had suggested to her that she maybe should give up one or more of her brood for adoption. Now there was a ninth mouth to feed.

I have no recollections of being deprived, but we must have been very poor. My sister Margaret remembers times when the house was dark and they went back to candles because the electricity had been cut off. And we suffered embarrassing moments at public school. Tuition was free, but parents were expected to provide the workbooks for their children. Margaret recalls how she hated hearing her name read aloud to the class for her to go to the headmaster's office to receive free workbooks. Each of her siblings quit school at 14 (the minimum age permitted by the state) in order to find work of any kind to help supplement the family income. Although my brothers and sisters did not lack in intelligence (several came to excel in business and professional fields), I was the only one who had the opportunity to complete secondary school.

Those years must have taken a terrible toll on my parents. Especially on my father, who wanted so much to work but could find no jobs.

Sometime during those years—I expect it was early into the Depression—Dad got an idea of making an opportunity for himself and the family. He would start a small business. He purchased a horse and cart, loaded it with supplies, and headed for the hills above Adelaide. There, on slopes and in gullies, often in isolated places and along back roads, farmers grew apples, pears, peaches, nectarines, cherries, grapes, and apricots.

I have only fuzzy memories of Dad's horse and cart. But years later he still had the metal cases he had used for his business, some of them still packed with items of clothing, toiletries, etc.

To the mind of children, life is a given. They don't know the struggle that adults have gone through to make their life possible. And so for many years I didn't think about what must have been the crucial question to Dad as he desperately sought to relieve the family's poverty. Where would he get the money to get started?

Some years after Dad's death I preached at an Adventist church in Albany, Western Australia. After the service an old gentleman wanted to talk to me. He'd known my father, and he wondered if I knew the story behind his little peddling business during the Depression. I listened in amazement.

Convinced that he had an idea that would work, Dad first went to his church for help. An elder and sometime member of the South Australia Conference committee, he was well known and respected. He told the treasurer of the conference of his need, but that leader shook his head sadly. "Brother Johnsson," he said, "we have no money to help you. Sorry."

Dad was now at his wit's end. He walked up and down the streets of Adelaide, racking his brains, no doubt imploring the Lord. He came upon the Methodist Mission and on an impulse went in. He met the head of the mission, Alan Broomhead, and told him his story. "I'm down on my luck," he said. "I want to work, but I can't get a job. I have a large family, and I don't want to go on the dole. Now, I have this plan . . ."

Broomhead listened in silence. Then he looked Dad straight in the eye and asked, "How much do you need to get started?"

"Fifty pounds." Dad must have choked at the words. Fifty pounds then would be thousands of dollars today and a huge amount in Depression terms.

Broomhead didn't say another word. He got up and went into another room. When he came back he put £50 in Dad's hands.

Dad was on his way. His business didn't bring in much, but something was a whole lot better than nothing. Even though he would be away weeks at a time, when he came home he had money in his pocket. And somehow we made it through to better times.

Broomhead's act was pure grace. No IOU. No lecture. No condescending attitude. No references.

You could even say Broomhead was reckless to hand out so much money to someone he'd never seen before, who'd just walked in off the street. But grace is reckless. Grace is irrational in terms of hard, cold economics. Grace takes chances. Grace goes out on a limb.

And all around us we see reckless people taking the same kind of chances Broomhead did. Parents. Teachers. People we've never met. Broomhead took a chance and helped me before I was even born. Scores of others along the way have taken a chance also. Some of them I know about; some I'm not even aware of.

These people take chances because God takes chances. God does it because that's the way He is—He simply takes chances. Others take chances because, ultimately, of what God did and does. This is the world of grace. It's wonderful, and it's ours.

Chapter Two

A BOY AND HIS HORSE

SOME PEOPLE TRY TO WRITE modern parables to help others discover grace. I'm not against such attempts, but I never met a modern parable that didn't leave me feeling it was a bit forced or even phony—something never true of Jesus' parables.

Others look for grace in novels. It's true that some great writers subtly but profoundly take us back—or forward—to grace, but you don't have to read novels to catch a glimpse of grace. Grace is all around us. The best stories and the clearest shafts of light on grace are right there in front of us.

Let me tell you about an amazing book—Monty Roberts' autobiography, *The Man Who Listens to Horses.* Some years earlier Monty's work with horses provided the key for the best-selling novel *The Horse Whisperer,* but the man himself has a better story than any novel.

Now, you need to realize that I'm not a horse person. I didn't grow up among horses, have never owned a horse, don't ride—and certainly don't follow the races! But for a long time I've been fascinated by the image of a horse at full speed—the long, sleek body; the flowing mane; the flaring nostrils; the big, soft eyes; the clattering hooves.

The Lord Himself takes delight in the glory of a horse. When He answered Job out of the storm, He said in part: "Do you give the horse his strength or clothe his neck with a flowing mane? Do you make him leap like a locust, striking terror with his proud snorting? He paws fiercely, rejoicing in his strength, and charges into the fray. He laughs at fear, afraid of nothing; he does not shy away from the sword. The quiver rattles against his side, along with the flashing spear and lance. In frenzied excitement he eats up the ground; he cannot stand still when the trumpet sounds. At the blast of the trumpet he snorts, 'Aha!' He catches the scent of battle from afar, the shout of commanders and the battle cry" (Job 39:19-25, NIV).

Unlike me, Monty Roberts grew up among horses. He was riding as soon as he could walk. By age 4 he was carrying home the trophy for equestrian events for kids 15 and younger. Horses became his life, still are. He worked as a stuntman in 100 or more Hollywood movies, filling in for big names, working alongside Shirley Temple and James Dean. A superb horseman, he won national contests in a range of exercises.

But Monty isn't only skilled in handling horses—he loves them. That's what impressed me most throughout his book: his admiration and respect for horses. Horses have been, and are, his closest companions and friends, and when they die he mourns for them with the grief of the loss of a bosom pal.

As great as is Monty's love for horses, it isn't unique. For thousands of years others have formed similar attachments. What sets him apart is the way he has endeavored to *understand* horses—how they communicate, to communicate with them, and ultimately to bond with them. This, the consuming passion of his life, has led to results so amazing, so extraordinary, that many doubt they can be true. But they are true, and Monty's efforts open to us a world that we didn't think possible, that we could only dream might exist after this life.

As a boy of 14 Monty spent hours on his belly while observing mustangs in the wilds of Nevada. He is totally color-blind, but his "disability" works to his advantage: he can discern details at great distances.

As the boy studied the mustangs from afar, he began to notice subtle signals of communication: the ear pointed up, the focus of the eyes, the head dropped low to the ground, the chewing motion. With amazement he watched the matriarch of the herd discipline an unruly colt, making him keep apart and unprotected until by silent language he indicated that he was sorry and was ready to be let back into the equine society.

Gradually an idea formed within the boy's head, one so radical that it would revolutionize the way humans approach horses. Instead of breaking colts by the use of force—with whip, rope, spur, and sharp bit as instruments—he would enter their world, gain their confidence, and win them to himself.

Monty's father, also a horseman, believed in the time-honored method. The only safe horse was one whose spirit had been forced to yield to a master, who had felt enough pain to be forever afraid of humans. Roberts senior would take as long as necessary—up to several weeks—and use whatever force it demanded to break a colt.

He wasn't about to accept a new method. His son's radical approach was stupid and dangerous. Unless a colt had been broken, it eventually would turn on riders and seek to maim or kill them. The relationship between horse and rider had to be slave and master, not mutual understanding and cooperation.

With mingled pride and apprehension the boy invited his father to witness his "gentling" of a wild colt through exercises designed to establish communication and build confidence. Within only 30 minutes the colt was approaching Monty for friendship and was ready to let him mount.

But the elder Roberts wasn't impressed. Taking a chain from the stable, he beat his son senseless: the boy had to be hospitalized.

If Monty's dad had hoped to break Monty's spirit in the same manner that he broke horses, his efforts backfired. More beatings followed and more hospitalizations, but the cruelty only strengthened the boy's resolve. He knew he was right, and one day the world would acknowledge it.

These were the years of World War II, and with the shortage

of men in the Salinas, California, area Monty's father took a job with the police force. One evening, unbeknown to his father, the boy saw his dad arrest a Black man caught in a petty robbery and proceed to knock him down and kick him in the head and chest with all his strength. The scene left an indelible mark in Monty's psyche. He determined that he would refuse to become like his father and would renounce the use of force against both humans and animals.*

How Monty broke away from his father's control, struggled to make it on his own, went through tough times but came out on top, makes a great story. Eventually his radical methods attracted attention, and he was featured in magazine write-ups. His method works—again and again, with now more than 10,000 horses that he has "gentled." He has succeeded with difficult horses that others couldn't master, restoring horses made crazy from fear and force. He has studied the silent language of horses and codified it— he calls it Equus.

The high point of his remarkable life came in the form of an extraordinary invitation. Elizabeth II, queen of the United Kingdom and herself a lover of horses, read about his work, became fascinated with its possibilities, and invited him to Windsor Castle. For a week he demonstrated his methods on a series of unbroken horses while the queen, Prince Philip, the queen mother, and assorted guests watched in astonishment. And the stable hands who came to mock slunk away in silence.

We look out on nature with ambivalent feelings. We like to camp in the wild and read up on what we need to do to ensure safety. We see beasts in the wild and admire them, but are glad for them to keep their distance.

Monty Roberts' work shatters our view of nature. It suggests that in our desire to have dominion over the animal kingdom, we have destroyed possibilities that we can hardly imagine today. It tells us that we can perhaps go much further than we thought possible toward realizing the otherworldly dream of a nature where "they will neither harm nor destroy on all my holy mountain" (Isa. 65:25, NIV).

By chance Monty Roberts got involved in helping an injured deer on the horse ranch he owns in southern California. He discovered that his method for horses also works with deer. He can lure deer out of the wild, win their trust, and have them bond with him.

The implications of this approach reach far beyond animals. Monty's work sheds light on interpersonal relationships—on learning to listen to one another, to read the silent signals, to understand, to build confidence, to establish trust. It tells us that not by force is the heart won—and certainly not by cleverness or trickery—but by love.

Listen to how God approaches us: "It was I who taught Ephraim to walk, taking them by the arms; but they did not realize it was I who healed them. I led them with cords of human kindness, with ties of love; I lifted the yoke from their neck and bent down to feed them" (Hosea 11:3, 4, NIV).

Did you notice the two beautiful images here? First, the parent and the toddler just beginning to walk. God, the loving Father, watches with delight at our first steps, taking our hands and catching us as we tumble.

Then God, the loving owner, leads His horses with cords of kindness, not a whip, lifting the burden from our shoulders and then bending down to feed us the bale of hay.

And that is grace. Grace is God loving us, helping us, delighting in us, catching us when we fall. Grace is God healing us, guiding us, liberating us, feeding us, stooping down to our level.

When Monty's father was an old man, his mother attempted to bring about a reconciliation between father and son, who had long been alienated. Under her cajoling and persuasion Dad at last grudgingly consented to spend time watching Monty at work "gentling" colts. The old man observed as horse after horse, untouched by humans, bonded with his son; observed how horses that would have taken him weeks to break were won in minutes.

A large part of the equestrian world by now was convinced, but not the critic whose opinion meant the most to Monty. At the end of the day his father uttered an exclamation of disbelief, warned Monty that he was courting suicide, and stalked away.

Grace is as close as the nose on your face, but you can go through life and not see it.

The other great disappointment of Monty's life came from an encounter with an eccentric millionaire. This man, excited by Monty's success in raising thoroughbreds, persuaded him to become a partner in establishing a world-class horse ranch in southern California. Monty was given the responsibility of setting up the ranch and its operation. It was hugely successful, and for several years Monty's wildest dreams seemed to have been realized.

But his partner was sick. He confided in Monty that his moods swung wildly from manic to depressive and that only heavy doses of medication enabled him to function. One day Monty's dream bubble burst. His partner wanted everything sold and the ranch broken up. And most diabolical of all, he ordered Monty personally to supervise the shooting of the finest horses.

According to the man's psychiatrist, he suffered from sand-castle syndrome. Like a child, he delighted in building the sand castle, but he equally delighted in seeing it swept away by the incoming tide. So he didn't just want the ranch sold—he wanted it uprooted, dismantled. And he wanted killed what had given him the highest pleasure, the horses.

Monty was appalled at the blinding turn of events. Unable to bring himself to destroy the horses, he had them secreted away.

And then the sky caved in on him. He felt the insane anger of a very rich man whose sadistic pleasure had been thwarted. Monty was arrested and handcuffed and thrown into a cell, man-acled to a ferocious giant of a man who would force him to confess to various misdeeds. But he survived the ordeal. Friends came to his aid, intervening with the authorities. After a protracted strug-gle the lawsuit brought against him was dropped, and Monty ended up owning the horse ranch.

This trying episode in Monty's life also provides a glimpse of grace. Force comes in a variety of forms, but love is stronger than violence, crooked cops, or madness. And in this world all people belong to just two classes—the builders and the wreckers. Those who belong to grace build up people, the church, society, the kingdom; all the others destroy.

In the life and work of Monty Roberts two worlds intersect. The first world is the one everyone takes for granted because it's so obvious and has always operated that way. But Monty caught a glimpse of another world—a kinder, gentler one that seems impossible to humans. Throughout the centuries a few people here and there had heard echoes of that world, but Monty opened his ears to hear its full-throated music. And he found and showed that the impossible was real and accessible.

These worlds are the worlds of force and fear on one hand, and of love and trust on the other.

_____

*A review of Monty Roberts' *The Man Who Listens to Horses* (*Time*, Dec. 14, 1998) acknowledges his amazing ability to "gentle" wild horses but questions the portrayal of his father. It casts doubt on the accounts of Monty's beatings and the incident with the Black soldier. The accusations come from Monty's younger brother Larry and others in the family circle. Having observed firsthand family dynamics and selective recall over time, I view these criticisms as interesting but unproven.

Chapter Three

THE GRACE STREAMER

HE CAME FROM HEAVEN TO earth, trailing streams of light. We call Him Jesus.

We are all like jet planes flying through the expanse of the heavens, leaving ribbons of white against the blue. Our jet trails—no matter how bright—blur, fade, and disappear, melting into the expanse as though we'd never been.

But His never fades. So long as the sky shall endure, as long as men and women have eyes to see, the divine imprint left by Jesus will blossom and glow. The centuries as they roll cannot dim it; the scoffing of critics cannot expunge it; the base neglect of those too blind to recognize cannot annul it.

Against that trail of light we measure every other life. Not our riches or fame, not our learning or degrees, not our accomplishments or our status count anymore—only the extent to which our little day in the noonday sun has in some small measure left a trail like His.

Jesus is too big to be contained in any word. John the Beloved said that if all the books that might be published about Him were written, they would amount to so many that the world could not contain them (John 21:25).

But there is a word that, better than any other, describes Jesus. Grace.

"The Word became flesh and made his dwelling among us. We have seen his glory, the glory of the One and Only, who came from the Father, *full of grace and truth*" (John 1:14, NIV).

The world has seen men and women of grace before and after Jesus, but none has ever been just like Him—full of grace.

Further, John tells us, "The law was given through Moses; grace and truth came through Jesus Christ" (verse 17, NIV). The two outstanding figures of the Scriptures: Moses in the Old, Jesus in the New. And the two outstanding events of the Scriptures: Sinai and Golgotha.

The Old Testament, written in Hebrew and Aramaic, has a wonderful word to describe God—*chesed.* Translated as mercy, love, loving-kindness, *chesed* portrays Yahweh, whose passion is His people, who can be counted on, who keeps covenant, who intervenes to help and to rescue.

But Jesus came, and human tongues fell silent. No word or words could capture the pure beauty and loveliness, the goodness and nobility, of this life. He came from heaven to earth, trailing streams of light.

His followers found a word—an old word, a word that went back a thousand years or more in Greek literature—and made it their own. Originally a secular, everyday term, it became Christian property, transformed because they applied it to Jesus. Once it was everyone's; now it became especially His, applied to all others only in a secondary, derivative sense.

Among the Greeks *charis* had various shades of meaning. It could refer to gratitude and thankfulness, just as we use the term when we say "grace" before eating. "Grace" could signify beauty, pleasantness, or favor, as in any attractive woman or amiable person.

But when Christians took *charis* and used it to describe Jesus, the word would never—could never—be the same again. He was *full* of it, so different from anyone who had come before that it was as though grace *came*—only began—with His appearance on earth.

What's the simplest definition of grace? Grace is a life; grace is a man—Jesus.

You look at the life of Jesus, try to see it whole—try to figure out what makes it so bright and enduring against the azure sky—and you are impressed with it as *active goodness.*

Jesus was always helping someone, always making the world a better place. At the end of every day someone was feeling better, had a better life. People who in the morning were crushed and broken, crippled with disease and burdened with care, had new hope and a new start.

"Jesus went throughout Galilee, teaching in their synagogues, preaching the good news of the kingdom, and healing every disease and sickness among the people. News about him spread all over Syria, and people brought to him all who were ill with various diseases, those suffering severe pain, the demon-possessed, the epileptics, and the paralytics, and he healed them. Large crowds from Galilee, the Decapolis, Jerusalem, Judea and the region across the Jordan followed him" (Matt. 4:23-25, NIV).

Jesus was a great teacher, but He gave His time to doing rather than to talking. He was, above all else, a healer. His passion for people—to help them, to uplift them, to liberate them—consumed Him.

It's true: No one ever spoke like Him, as even His enemies acknowledged (John 7:46). But His words had power and rang with truth because of what He did—He lived what He spoke. Summing up Jesus' life, Peter said: "God anointed Jesus of Nazareth with the Holy Spirit and power, and he went around doing good and healing all who were under the power of the devil" (Acts 10:38, NIV).

Jesus was unalloyed goodness, goodness through and through.

To that add *compassion.* He saw the crowds, broken and harried, and His heart cried out for them. He saw the leper, cut off from society, banished outside the camp, longing to be clean, and He reached out and touched him. He saw the widow, the light of her life snuffed out with the death of her only child, and He gave her back her son. He saw Mary and Martha grieving over the death of Lazarus, and He wept with them and brought back their brother from the grave.

And *thoughtfulness*. Jesus was always looking out for the faceless people, the little people, the neglected people. He made it a point to notice and help the weak and the powerless and the social outcastes. He invited women to His table, installed them as disciples. He welcomed children and mothers with infants. He sat down to eat with tax-gatherers and assorted sinners. He didn't care about being politically correct, being seen with the right kind of people, saying the right kind of things. Samaritans and ladies of the night, Zacchaeuses and Magdalenes, as well as Nicodemuses— they all got His attention. The only test was human need.

Goodness, compassion, thoughtfulness, kindness—that's Jesus. Alongside His life, Buddha, Zoroaster, and Muhammad can't hold a candle.

Yet we have to go further. Jesus as grace personified exhibits something even more startling. In Him we see goodness, compassion, and thoughtfulness more than in any other; but we also see something that's not just *more* than but is startlingly different.

Jesus' life reverses the social order. Jesus turned on its head the way people were used to relating to one another—and still does.

Listen to the way men and women relate to each other in our world, and you hear two expressions that sum up society: "He owes me one" and "I'll get even."

When we say "He owes me one," we mean that we've helped someone in some way, done a favor for them, and that they're obligated to return the favor. One good turn deserves another. Every act on behalf of another accumulates points. We build up a stockpile of merit with someone else. By helping others we've put them in our debt.

That's the way the world works. It's as up-to-date as Wall Street deals, but as ancient as pagan religion. The devotee brought an offering and placed it before the god on the same principle: I've given to you; now you must give to me—protection, children, health, whatever. You owe me one.

The amazing, striking thing about Jesus is that, for all His kind deeds to others, He never said, "You owe Me one." He never put conditions on the sick, the poor, the hungry, or the broken before He would help them. The only "condition" was their need—that was enough for Him.

When the down-and-outers came to Jesus' soup kitchen, He didn't make them listen to a sermon before He brought out the food.

When those who were blind or deaf or disabled came to Him for healing, He didn't ask them to sign the pledge before He made them whole.

When the disgraced and the shamed crept to Him, He didn't say, "I'll help you if you'll help yourself and get your life on track."

True, by the Pool of Bethesda He did tell the man who'd been crippled for 38 years, "Stop sinning or something worse may happen to you" (John 5:14, NIV), but that was *after* He healed him, not before. And He did tell the woman caught in adultery, "Go now and leave your life of sin," but that was *after* He assured her, "Neither do I condemn you" (John 8:11, NIV).

From one point of view, Jesus was reckless in His generosity. He simply gave and gave and gave without prescreening or tests or computer checks. That sounds like courting disaster, encouraging people to expect a handout.

In fact, it's the divine way of changing people—and the world.

Jesus told His followers to deal with others in just the same way. When you give to someone, He said, don't select those people who will pay you back. Treat people just as you would like them to treat you. Love your enemies and lend to them, not expecting to get it back (Luke 6:32-36).

As far-out as this advice sounds, it was actually the way Jesus lived. Once when He was invited to a party (He was a popular dinner guest) He looked around and noticed who was there—the wealthy and influential, the high society of Jerusalem. Then He told the host, "Next time you have a party, don't invite your friends and the big shots. Instead, invite the little people, the ones out on the margins, who will never invite you back. Invite the blind, the lame, the crippled—people who wouldn't dare to come near your gate" (Luke 14:12-14, paraphrased).

They were the people Jesus invited to His party. He threw open the doors of new life to anyone and everyone who wanted in. No one was too rich or too poor, too powerful or too weak, too confident or too broken, to have a place at His table.

He especially faulted the "religious" people of His day—the scribes and Pharisees—because they made so much of appearances. They did a lot of good, but they always made sure the world knew about it. For any charitable gift, any act of mercy, any prayer or pious deed they expected a return—that others would see and applaud their generosity and devotion and that God would put it down in His credit ledger.

In word and life Jesus totally rejected the owe-me philosophy. The outpouring of goodness, kindness, thoughtfulness, and compassion that was His life came with no strings, no fine print, no bottom line. He gave and gave and gave without conditions.

That was the way He lived; that was the way He died. From a human standpoint, which weighs the return on the investment, the cross was recklessly wasteful, an incredible miscalculation. Here is the Ruler of the universe offering men and women the greatest gift of all time, and what do they do with it? They spit in His face, turn and walk away, leaving God hanging on the cross.

But here is the mystery and the marvel we call grace: *Jesus would have gone to His death if only one person had accepted the gift and all the billions of people born since Adam had walked away.*

In fact, grace goes even further. *Jesus would have died for everyone even if no one responded!*

Grace doesn't count numbers. Grace doesn't count the cost. Grace doesn't figure return on investment. Grace doesn't keep a score of the good done for others and the good they've done in return.

Nor does grace keep a score of wrongs.

I picked up an interview with Donald Trump one evening on television. Successful, confident, wealthy, he made it clear to the

TV host that getting even played a big part in his thinking. Don't mess with Donald Trump if you don't want to get hurt!

A friend recounted a conversation he had with a Serbian Christian. He listened in mounting concern and horror to a litany of atrocities inflicted by the Croats: rape, torture, mutilation, killings. The scenes from Bosnia that played out for years on the evening news flashed before his eyes, and his heart went out to his friend, whose dear ones had suffered such monstrosities.

He inquired as to which relatives his friends had lost, and then the light dawned—his friend was describing events from 150 years ago! But they were so real, so vivid, to the Serb that he wept and wailed as he recounted them.

You could talk to a Croat and have the identical conversation, except that the atrocities were perpetrated by the Serbs just as long ago, or longer. Here are two peoples who look the same, whose language is almost identical, who have lived in proximity and who to some extent have intermarried, but each people retains memories that span the centuries and keep an unrelenting score. Under the iron hand of Tito they were forced to live in uneasy truce, but the dictator's demise released a bloodletting. Each act of savagery, each murder, each strike of retaliation, expiated nothing. They only added to the grim lists calling out for blood.

The mindless carnage of Bosnia has been repeated over and over in human history as people and nations wait for payback time.

India, 1947: On the stroke of midnight on August 15 the nation threw off the yoke of British rule. But freedom came at a terrible price. The subcontinent was carved into new boundaries without regard to geography, and the two regions where Muslims predominate, although separated by nearly 1,000 miles, became Pakistan. One of the largest displacements in human history transpired as millions of Indian Hindus were uprooted and millions of Indian Muslims replaced them.

Violence erupted. People were hurt, some killed. Centuries-long resentments burst forth. Both Hindus and Muslims no longer regarded those of the other religion as human beings. "Hindu" and

"Muslim" became tags that justified unrestrained savagery. Every Muslim who lost a relative in the mayhem determined to pay back Hindus—with interest. And so did each Hindu on the other side. Madness continued to reign; freedom flowed in rivers of blood. Trains pulled into the central station in New Delhi, but no one emerged; attendants looked in and saw whole carriages filled with corpses—bodies shot, stabbed, and hacked to death by posses bent on vengeance at stops along the way. When the slaughter finally subsided, millions had died—no one really knows how many.

Rwanda, 1994: Another time, another continent, but the same ghastly scenes were replayed as Hutus, long chafing under the rule of the Tutsi minority, seized power and exacted a terrible price for years of oppression, real or imagined, but etched in the corporate memory. Butchered bodies floated down the river, fouled the waters of Lake Victoria. Again masses bundled up their belongings and fled for safety. Now it wasn't Hindu against Muslim and Muslim against Hindu, but Christian against Christian—even as it has been in Bosnia and Northern Ireland.

We could go on: Arabs against Jews, and Jews against Arabs. In the United States—not the extent of savagery but savagery nevertheless—Whites against Blacks, and Blacks against Whites. Time was when no Southern jury would bring down a guilty verdict for a White man's atrocity against a Black. Is it any wonder that the Los Angeles jury in O. J. Simpson's first trial acquitted him after minimal deliberation?

Problems like those in the Middle East, Rwanda, and Northern Ireland grind on and on, defying solution, wearying the spirit, sapping the creative energies. Similarly internal disputes within congregations—families that harbor grudges against other families, people who won't talk to others—quench the Spirit and derail the church from its mission.

Some problems are so ingrained in human relationships, have become so much a part of human nature, that humanly they can never be solved. Only a power that comes from outside of us, that takes the problem and transforms it, can break the cycle. A power that helps us see that violence will never remove violence, hate remove hate, suspicion remove suspicion, one score of wrongs remove another score of wrongs.

That power is wonderful, and it's real. It's divine. It enables us to wipe the slate clean and start over. It brings forgiveness, a new start. It points to a future instead of a past, to love instead of hate, to acceptance instead of rejection.

That power is grace.

That power is Jesus, the Grace Streamer. Listen to how He reacted at payback time: "'He committed no sin, and no deceit was found in his mouth.' When they hurled their insults at him, he did not retaliate; when he suffered, he made no threats. Instead, he entrusted himself to him who judges justly. He himself bore our sins in his body on the tree, so that we might die to sins and live for righteousness; by his wounds you have been healed" (1 Peter 2:22-24, NIV).

Grace gives, and grace forgives.

Chapter Four

WORLD WITHOUT GRACE

WHAT WOULD A WORLD WITHOUT grace be like? I saw it once, and I hated it with a passion.

In 1982 the General Conference arranged three Bible conferences for our ministers in Europe. One was held at our college at Collonges in southern France, one at our Marienhoehe Seminary near Darmstadt in West Germany, and one at Friedensau, the Adventist seminary behind the iron curtain in East Germany.

The entire month of meetings left an indelible impression on me, but the conference that stands out was the one at Friedensau. I wanted to write about it as soon as I returned to the office, but the political realities of the times—the well-being of our workers under the yoke of Communism—dictated that I bite my tongue.

Some 300 ministers jammed to overflowing the facilities of Friedensau. They came from East Germany, Poland, Hungary, Romania, Czechoslovakia, even a few from the Soviet Union itself. I experienced their hunger to learn, their depth of devotion, their exuberant singing, their love. As we washed one another's feet, I felt the joy of Christian fellowship and the bonding of the Holy Spirit. I looked into their lovely, lean faces and saw for the first time in my life the suffering church.

Friedensau accommodations were basic and the food meager. (As a big favor—and after much discussion—the authorities granted us a cheese ration for the conference!) But the campus was an oasis of light and joy, a Shangri-la where grace reigned in a graceless land.

I loved Friedensau, but I hated everything else about East Germany.

We went through the iron curtain in East Berlin. Getting through immigration was long and tedious. We were taken individually into little booths with mirrors behind and above us. Grim-faced agents went through our papers again and again. Then other agents checked them yet one more time. Not a smile, not a welcoming word. We had the distinct sense that they didn't want us in their country and were trying to find some flaw in the papers, some technicality, so that they could boot us out.

Suspicion. That was my first impression of this world without grace. In this world you were always suspect. In fact, everyone was suspect. It was a world where everyone spied on everyone else, right to the very top. If you made it there, you had to walk with eyes in your back, forever wondering who was out to get you and roll you in the dust.

It was a *phony* world. You couldn't be yourself. You had to toe the party line and mouth the party platitudes. The German Democratic Republic, they called it, wearing their phoniness right on their sleeve. Beware of any country that has to insert the word "Democratic" in its official name, because you can bet your boots that democracy is one quality you *won't* find there!

I recall Alexander Solzhenitsyn's accounts of party congresses in the old Soviet Union. The big shot would stand up and drone on and on for hours with boring platitudes, and when at last he finished, the clapping would begin. A minute, and they were still clapping. Two minutes. Three minutes. No stopping—sometimes 10 minutes, and no one dared to stop. The secret police were watching, waiting to see who stopped first and to note the names in their files.

We drove through East Berlin in the tiny, puttering, sputtering Trabant car owned by the president of the German Democratic

Republic Union, Elder Boettcher. We saw wide streets with hardly any vehicles. We saw the concrete monoliths erected by the Communist regime and another fact hit us: *ugly!*

A world without grace is an ugly world. When the human spirit is pressed into an ideological mold, when every creation of the hand or the mind has to pass the test of political correctness, you won't find anything lovely or beautiful. Nothing playful, nothing fun. A deathly pall falls over all of life.

For 75 years the Soviet Union embraced Communism. For nearly 50 of those years it held sway over a vast empire of nations stretching from the Danube to the Sea of Japan. What lasting works of art—visual or in sound—remain from that era? Almost nothing. It was perhaps the most artistically barren empire in human history.

In one arena only did the graceless world appear to excel—athletics. The Soviet Union, and East Germany in particular, hauled away barrel-loads of gold medals from the Olympic Games. But the young people who won the gold had been made puppets of the state—selected at an early age, separated, programmed, trained relentlessly. They were soldiers rather than athletes in the Olympic spirit. They were commandos with a mission in the cold war. And, we now know, many of the records they set were made possible by the use of banned substances. The phoniness of the world without grace extended even to the Olympics.

It was a world of *force.* We saw groups of German police in their ill-fitting gray uniforms patrolling the streets of Berlin, eyes alert, guns at the ready. Occasionally we saw groups of equally surly and grim Russian soldiers in their drab green outfits.

Welcome to a world without grace!

The leader of East Germany had built what he thought would be a showpiece—a revolving restaurant. But when the afternoon sun hit it, it made the form of a cross, and the people—behind closed doors—quickly dubbed it "Honecker's cathedral."

We took the elevator up to the observation deck. Hundreds had gathered there before us and were clustered on the western side, looking out to where people lived in freedom. Freedom was just a few miles away, but barring it was the ugliest sight I've ever seen. The wall snaked through the city, dividing family from family and friend from friend. On one side the people lived right up to the wall. On this, the eastern side, the housing had been removed and a deadly no-man's-land had been put in place with barbed wire, attack dogs, and sentries at the ready.

Everywhere we went in East Berlin we saw posters and billboards proclaiming the greatness of socialism and the doom of capitalism. Great, all right, when you have to wall your citizens in so that they won't leave!

It was a world of *fear.* You always lived on the edge. You never knew when the knock might come on your door at midnight and the bright lights turned on so that the neighbors would see and tremble. You or a loved one would be hauled away and maybe never seen again. You never knew if some chance remark, some careless word about the authorities, had been overheard and reported by someone you thought was a friend. You never knew when you might find yourself dispossessed, ostracized, bullied, accused, tortured, sentenced.

Perhaps the hardest aspect of life in that world without grace was the state's relationship to your children. Our leaders didn't want to talk much about it to us—it was too painful. The state viewed children as their property. So if you didn't send them to school on Sabbath, the state would take them from you. What would *you* do if faced with that choice?

Somehow, wonderfully, our people survived those unimaginable years. They clung to God and to one another. The state let them have their music, and Adventist music flourished. And the state let them keep Friedensau for training of pastors. Here, in this oasis of grace in a graceless world, our people would gather for spiritual retreats and instruction. They would vacation here and sit in classes to learn more about the Bible. They would send their children here for spiritual nurture and instruction. And slowly the long night passed.

Their lives were shackled, but their spirits were free. Quietly, in secret, they not only built up one another in Christ, but also the well of creativity born of grace bubbled up in humor. Because their hope was not in this world, because they knew their God, they could laugh at the stupidity and phoniness and posturing of the state. After a few days at Friedensau, when they had looked us over and decided they could trust us, some of them told us the jokes that made the rounds in secret. Without exception they lampooned the most obvious symbols of the regime—the police and the Russians.

I believe God is calling the Advent people to manifest His grace. Says Ellen White: "The last rays of merciful light, the last message of mercy to be given to the world, is a revelation of His character of love. The children of God are to manifest His glory. In their own life and character they are to reveal what the grace of God has done for them" (Christ's Object Lessons, pp. 415, 416).

That means we must not only proclaim but live.

Let the Advent people be a people of trust, not suspicion.

Let us be real, not phony.

Let the beauty of Christ be seen manifested among us, not the ugliness of self.

Let love, not force, be our guiding rule.

Let joy cast out all fear among us.

Let us walk in the freedom of Christ, who died to set the world free.

We were in East Germany for only a week, but it seemed like forever. I loved the people but hated this stifling, graceless world.

At the close of the conference several of us took speaking assignments at various churches in the Berlin area. We had strict instructions to be careful what we said, that informers would be present to take note of every word.

After the Sabbath, Bill Shea and I were taken to a hotel to spend the night prior to our departure on the morrow. Our room was tiny and spartan, with two narrow beds, one against each wall. But the room had a radio, and before long we found the band for the American Armed Forces. We turned up the volume till the room reverberated and, figuring our quarters were bugged, shouted out messages urging whoever might be listening in to enjoy the sound of freedom.

The next morning we packed our bags and got in the elevator. Again, assuming the elevator was bugged, we spoke to the ceiling and told someone—or no one—how good life was beyond the wall.

Bags in hand, we walked to Checkpoint Charlie. It was the same grim scene as when we'd arrived: surly, unsmiling officials; endless scrutiny of documents; suspicion and hostility so thick in the air you could cut it with a knife. They took our documents, put us in a small room, and triggered the electronic lock. After a long wait they let us out, only to send us a few yards along to another room where again the door went *zing!* as it flew shut behind us. Would we ever get out of here? Would we ever get our passports back?

At last all the officials involved had checked enough and consulted enough to cover their hides, and they felt safe to let us go. We were out of there without a word—no "Thank you, come again" (as if we would!), no smile, no human courtesy.

Dragging our cases, we came to a line across the road. We looked up and saw, instead of slogans vaunting the triumph of socialism, neon signs and billboards for Coke and McDonald's.

Then—a checkpoint on the right, with a U.S. marine standing by it. Instinctively we reached for our passports as he headed toward us. But he gave us a big grin and waved us on. "Welcome to freedom!" he said.

And—I kid thee not—it was the Fourth of July.

Chapter Five

DR. MAC

WHEN I TAUGHT AT THE seminary, one summer they asked me to go to Europe and conduct extension classes for ministers in France and Germany. Joining me from the General Conference Health Department was a guest lecturer, Dr. Wayne McFarland. The two months we spent together were, as Humphrey Bogart might have said, the beginning of a wonderful friendship.

Ever notice how you just seem to "click" with some people? How you find yourself trading wisecracks even though you've hardly met?

It happened from day one, and it's never stopped. We may not see each other for several years, but as soon as we get together something goes off inside our heads.

Actually, we have little in common. For a start, there's the disparity in our ages—he's at least 40 years older. Further, we look very different—he's a little, wizened gnome of a man. His wife, Dolly, has to be a saint to put up with him. As if all this weren't enough, he's a quack wedded to the practice of smoke and mirrors they call medicine. I, on the other hand, have followed the queen of sciences—theology—and the noble call of the ministry.

Yet somehow we get along—oh, do we get along!

Doctor Mac is the merriest person I know, and for me it's a joy just to be around him.

In fairness I need to tell you that he did find one or two worthwhile things to do with his life. Apart from serving at the General Conference, he taught at Temple University, Thomas Jefferson University, and Loma Linda University. He edited our health journal and wrote articles and books. He coinvented the Five Day Plan to Stop Smoking—the first program of its kind anywhere. Of course, I was only a boy when he did all this. He kept working until he was really old—probably to give Dolly a break from having to see him the whole day through—but even after he retired and is now in his 80s he still makes trips to exotic places such as Russia and China to help people give up the pernicious weed.

Humor is a funny thing. And very tricky also: HANDLE WITH CARE needs to start flashing every time we get into it. Humor easily cuts and wounds or becomes the prattle of fools.

But the world is funny. So are people. Methinks God gave us humor to help us bear the pain and tragedy that might otherwise engulf us. And also to remind us that He is good and not evil, that the world—despite its mess—is still a jolly good place, so why not enjoy it? It's God's world, after all.

Humor is a gift of grace.

From the time Doctor Mac and I first taught together that summer, grace was in our hearts and on our lips as much as the wisecracks. I offered my seminary course "Law, Grace, and Freedom"; he taught "Ministry of Healing." The courses were made for each other, and fit together in a manner totally unforeseen and totally delightful.

Because I was the full-time seminary teacher, I was responsible for seeing that Wayne's grades got to Shahin Ilter in the graduate records office. And I couldn't help noticing that Doctor Mac had a grading system unlike any that I'd ever come across and that would challenge Shahin's considerable powers.

As Doctor Mac was working through the students' examination papers, he was pleased enough with the work to award several A grades. Then he came upon a couple of others that were even better, so they received an A+ designation. But that wasn't the end of it. One or two papers that were clearly superior to all the others came along, so what to do? They got A++. And—you guessed it—later in the pile the crème de la crème appeared. Only one grade possible: A+++. It was, I daresay, one of the most interesting grade sheets ever turned in at Andrews University.

Maybe those grades told as much about the teacher as they did about his students. Wayne McFarland has such a cheery, positive attitude toward the world and its people that you have to really blow it not to be A class in his book. Is that what grace does to us when it becomes a living reality and not just a theory?

During those months together in Europe, Wayne and I walked and talked a lot together. We walked because we didn't have a car—walked up the road to the top of the Saleve, where cowbells tinkled in meadows thick with flowers and hang gliders leaped off the cliff and floated down to land in Switzerland; walked down to the road and to the border, where we caught a bus and then a trolley to Geneva, where we bought a copy of the *Herald Tribune* and gelato cones and then took the trolley and bus back and walked up the long hill to the college.

We walked and talked and laughed. We laughed over the lack of hot water: A busload of Andrews students came through on tour and ran out all the hot water, and those of us who stayed on were limited to cold only for a week. We laughed over some of the food offerings. We laughed over the foibles of humanity and the sheer fun of God's good world.

The combination of our classes—grace and health—seemed to work so well that we began to dream about an evangelistic approach different from anything either of us had ever seen. A few years later we tried it out in a miniseries—just a week—in the Grantham church in England. I spoke each night from the Sermon on the Mount, and Wayne gave a health message. The meetings went well, and while we can't claim spectacular numbers, at least one baptism resulted.

For several years after that, Wayne entertained hopes of a larger effort in the land of his forebears—Scotland. The Adventist message has struggled there from the beginning. Today only about 250 members can be found on the church rolls, but the actual number attending Sabbath services is far fewer. The sad fact is that Adventism is dying out in Scotland.

There people follow the old ways, and the Presbyterian Church holds sway. Since the usual approaches to evangelism consistently fail, Wayne thought that our grace-health team thrust might provide the breakthrough. He settled on Aberdeen on the northeast coast, where a small congregation meets in a little chapel each Sabbath. The pastor was receptive to our emphasis. After juggling with dates, we eventually found three weeks in May that fit Wayne's and my schedules.

The pastor secured the finest venue in the city, the music hall, for a two-day health fair, and sought out qualified Adventists from around Scotland and England to join us in conducting blood pressure screening, lung capacity tests, and so on. But in trying to arrange for the complicated program, he somehow slipped up on a vital aspect—advertising. Wayne and I arrived in Aberdeen a couple of days before the health fayre was due to open, and found disaster. The city hadn't been told about it.

Then the Lord did something wonderful. A radio station heard about the fayre—the first in the city's history—and began broadcasting free announcements. When the doors of the music hall opened, people were lined up by the hundreds. More than 1,000 came to the event during the two days, an unprecedented response to an Adventist initiative in Scotland.

The plan was to enroll people who came to the fayre in a series of seminars—"How to Stop Smoking," "Spiritual Life," "Stress Control," and so on. On the closing night of the two-day event we would have a public lecture right in the main hall, with Doctor Mac speaking about the physiology of stress and me wrapping up the evening with a spiritual emphasis. On subsequent nights we'd continue in a smaller room of the music hall, and finally move to the Adventist chapel for the seminars commencing the following week.

Problem: I came down with a bug that knocked me flat just as the fayre was to begin. I'd come up from England, where I'd spent a week speaking at the North England Conference camp meeting, held that year at the seaside resort of Scarborough. Kind folk had met me at Heathrow Airport, driven me to the campsite, and ensconced me in a nice warm room. But that first night, tired as I was from jet lag, I woke up in the pitch darkness. The room was freezing—I couldn't get warm. Only the next day did I discover the reason—I hadn't fed tokens into the heater to keep the warmth flowing.

One week later, feeling terrible and barking like a dog, I got down from the train at Aberdeen station. When the fayre opened, I tried to help for a few hours but gave up and went to bed, where, so congested that I could hardly speak, I stayed throughout the next day. And that night I was supposed to bat cleanup for Wayne in the opening meeting. Again the Lord came through, as He always does. I got up that evening and was able to present the topic with little apparent impairment.

The next evening we moved to a smaller room in the music hall. By now the local pastor was also in bed sick, and Wayne and I experienced what it's like to do evangelism in a small church. You do *everything,* from putting out the chairs, introducing yourself, welcoming the people, to greeting them at the close. The president of the Scottish Mission showed up to give us a boost. After the service he thanked us and with a "Cheerio, chaps" (or equivalent) and tootled off in his Rover. We put away the chairs, locked up, and headed out into the night—on foot, since we couldn't find any other transport.

A bitterly cold wind cut through my overcoat as if it were paper as we walked the two miles to the bed-and-breakfast where we were staying. All the way Wayne talked and laughed, and I laughed and coughed.

Wayne and I shared a room in the bed-and-breakfast. Through the night I tossed and hack-hack-hacked, while Wayne tossed and listened. Sometime during the wee hours he got up and went out. I heard the sound of water running in the bathroom down the hallway. When he returned he put on the light, came over to my bed, and said, "All right, I want you to take off your pajama top and undershirt and lie flat on your stomach."

Whack! I leaped up as a steaming hot towel came down on my skin. Then *wham!* I leaped again as a freezing cold twin repeated it. For the next 30 or 40 minutes Wayne went back and forth, in and out, alternating hot and cold, until the bugs in my system decided it was time to seek more comfortable quarters.

All the while Wayne kept up a patter. "For years I've waited to put some heat on the clergy," he muttered. Then he started singing words he composed on the spot to the tune of "She'll Be Comin' 'Round the Mountain": "O we'll roast 'em and we'll toast 'em, yes, we will . . ." So in the dead of the night he was roasting and freezing me and laughing, and I was leaping and squirming and laughing.

And loving him all the more.

When the torture was over, we both slept happily ever after.

Doctor Mac—what a man! A man of love and merriment, a man of grace. We'd be having lunch at a restaurant down the street from the music hall, and the other patrons would be looking at us and wondering what we were drinking so that they could order a bottle. The waitresses would come hovering over Wayne, which I could never figure out, since he was so old and ugly, and soon he'd be telling them about the meetings and inviting them to come along. We'd be walking down the streets of Aberdeen, and Wayne would point out the distinctive features of adults born with fetal alcohol syndrome, and we'd sorrow together at the ravages of whiskey in the land of John Knox. We'd be eating supper at the bed-and-breakfast before the evening meeting, and the other guests would be cracking up. Our genial Scottish host, laughing, would call out, in his thick brogue, "You gentlemen ought to be on the telly!"

Once I called Doctor Mac at his home in southern California.

The long-suffering Dolly answered the telephone, and I swore her to secrecy as she called Wayne to the line.

"Doctor," I said, trying to disguise my voice, "I've got this terrible back. What do you suggest I do about it?"

Without a pause and in a level voice the reply came back: "You need to find a place where they're doing roadwork. When you see the steam roller coming, lie down flat on your face, and let it iron out your back."

Only when I exploded did Doctor Mac break into a laugh.

Chapter Six

WHAT I LEARNED ABOUT GRACE FROM KIDS...

OK, THE SHOE IS ON THE other foot. We are the learners and the kids our teachers.

Jesus loved kids, and they loved Him. They came to Him, climbed onto His lap, cradled their heads on His shoulder, felt His big arms hugging them. Jesus loved them because they were—kids.

Jesus said things about kids that His adult followers have been trying to explain and explain away ever since. Peter, James, John, and the other disciples sought to prevent the kids from coming to Jesus. We try to ignore what He said about them.

But here's what He said: "I tell you the truth, unless you change and become like little children, you will never enter the kingdom of heaven" (Matt. 18:3, NIV). Overruling the disciples, who wanted to keep the kids away, He said: "The kingdom of heaven belongs to such as these" (Matt. 19:14, NIV). On another occasion He prayed, "I praise you, Father, Lord of heaven and earth, because you have hidden these things from the wise and learned, and revealed them to little children" (Matt. 11:25, NIV).

On that final Sunday of His life Jesus rode in triumph into Jerusalem. He healed the blind and the lame, and the children shouted in the Temple, "Hosanna to the Son of David" (Matt. 21:15, NIV). Indignant, the chief priests and teachers of the law demanded, "Do you hear what these children are saying?" (verse 16, NIV).

"'Yes,' replied Jesus, 'have you never read, "From the lips of children and infants you have ordained praise?"'" (verse 16, NIV).

I believe Jesus meant just what He said. Children are closer to the kingdom of heaven than adults. Only as we become like them do we enter it.

Noelene and I have been blessed with two children, Terry and Julie, both born in India. Here's what I've learned from them and other kids about grace.

1. Grace means being happy just to receive.

The smaller the child, the greater this truth. Infants are totally dependent. Their world consists of eating, sleeping, and diaper changes. They're constantly receiving and are content to do so.

We bring them gifts—stuffed toys and rattles and bright colored objects that twinkle and turn. We hover by the crib, crooning and singing, trying to tease out a smile or a giggle. And baby lies and watches and soaks in the adult attention, feeling the love, secure and content.

Then, holding her head without wobbling, sitting up, creeping across the floor, crawling, pulling herself up onto wobbly legs, she takes her first steps. And there's the first Christmas, and the first birthday. Parties and presents wrapped in paper with pretty bows. Toys that move and speak and sing.

Then another year and another birthday and another Christmas. Balls and bats, tricycles and training wheels, and bicycles. The years fly by, but they stay the same—years of giving, years of receiving.

We adults—yes, even we adults who profess to be followers of Jesus—find it hard to receive like that. Every religion across the face of the earth tells you to *first* give to the Deity and then the Deity will give back to you. Present your offering, make that pilgrimage, wash and make yourself clean, follow the formula. Then

God will do for you what you seek.

But Jesus came along and said, "Just receive. Open your arms wide. Stretch out those chubby little fingers. Simply take what I offer you."

Listen to Ellen White saying the same thing: "To him who is content to receive without deserving, who feels that he can never recompense such love, who lays all doubts and unbelief aside, and comes as a little child to the feet of Jesus, all the treasures of eternal love are a free, everlasting gift" (*Signs of the Times,* Feb. 28, 1906).

2. Grace means giving without guilt.

One of the best Christmas gifts I ever received came from a little child—my son, Terry.

We were far from home on Christmas Eve, far from the sounds of carols and evergreens and colored lights, far from stores packed with shining gifts and crowds rushing to complete their shopping in anticipation of the holidays with family and dear ones. In Hindu India, December 25 comes and goes, and you might never know it.

It was Christmas Eve, and my thoughts turned home to Adelaide in southern Australia. I remembered the hills above the city and the delicious apples that grow on their slopes. How I longed to bite into a crisp, juicy Jonathan apple!

"I'll get you an apple, Daddy," said Terry, and he scurried off. He returned, eyes shining, with something cradled in his fist. He opened his hand and presented me with—a large red marble!

We all laughed at the fun—and the beauty—of his thought. Just so, the carol about the little drummer boy who has nothing to give but plays his best still tugs at our hearts.

It's undeniable. We adults are all messed up when it comes to giving. Look at the season that of all times of the year focuses on gifts and presents. But instead of grace and goodwill, Christmas has become the season of guilt and greed.

Look at the crowds worrying about *what* (what do you give to people who already have more than they need?) and *how much?* (if

I spend too little, they'll think I'm stingy; if I spend more than they spend on me, they'll think I'm uppity).

If you need any evidence that our giving has gone to seed, visit a shopping mall as the hours wind down on Christmas Eve. See the harried, nervous, last-minute buyers; see the robot-like, glassy-eyed checkout clerks.

We no longer know how to give with grace. But we can learn from little children.

3. *Grace means receiving with joy.*

You've seen it: Eager parents and friends gather around for the opening of the birthday presents, and the kid blows it. While the adults are oohing and aahing over the big fancy gizmo and making quick mental calculations about the cost, the baby turns from the toy and becomes engrossed in the wrapping paper.

Kids, especially little ones, don't have expectations about gifts. They don't measure according to what the other kid received or the dollar tag. They don't feel guilty because they don't have an equivalent gift to return.

They simply have a good time with whatever they receive. They can receive with joy.

One year in India Noelene and I planned a really special Christmas. We'd been in the United States on furlough and had brought back a snow-white faux tree with bright-blue balls for decorations. With high expectations we set it up in the living room and placed the kids' presents underneath. By American standards it was a modest tree, with gifts modest in number and size, but it was attractive and different enough in India for the local newspaper to send out a photographer.

On Christmas Eve Terry came down with a fever. Noelene and I were up late caring for him and making last-minute preparations for the big day to come. We overslept on Christmas morning, awaking with the sense that something definitely wasn't right in the house. The sight in the living room that met our eyes confirmed it.

Terry and Julie were surrounded with piles of torn-off wrappings, and they were playing with their new toys. We'd planned to take lots of pictures of the opening of gifts, but all I got was a heavy-eyed boy and his sister in a scene of chaos.

Noelene and I were upset, and we let the kids know it. In retrospect, however, we began to wonder if we'd overreacted, if by being so concerned for our pleasure on Christmas morning we'd lost the meaning of the gift-opening event.

They were good kids and meant no harm by their actions. If we hadn't built up the occasion so much and then slept in, they wouldn't have gone ahead without us. They were closer to the spirit of Christmas than we were.

It's hard to give without strings and mental IOUs. It's hard to receive without deserving—as kids do.

4. Grace means forgiving and forgetting.

Little children don't bear grudges. No chips on their shoulders, no score of wrongs and slights.

Our best efforts as parents fall woefully short. Often our very concern to do what's best for the kids makes us uptight and unreasonable. Our ego gets in the way, and the kids suffer.

But God has put amazing resiliency within children. Every now and then we read about a child who defies all the odds—someone from the ghetto, someone whose mother was a prostitute, someone whose future seems carved in relenting stone from the day of birth, dooming the youngster to failure—but who rises above the environment and leaves us with mouths agape.

That resiliency enables kids to overlook our failures and shortcomings as parents. They love us in spite of us rather than because of us. They forgive, wipe the slate clean, and start over.

Growing up and entering the world hardens us. We learn about bullies; we learn about fear; we learn about survival. We lose trust; we gain experience. We divide our world into those who are safe for us and those who aren't. And even when we forgive, we transfer the name and event to our mental computer file.

Jesus' kingdom reverses the hardening. It takes us back to where we started—experienced now, yes, but with the open heart of a little child.

5. Grace means the obedience of poverty.

Look at the little child surrounded by parents and relatives showering gifts. What does the child have to give in return? What *can* the child give?

And look at us surrounded by a loving heavenly family showering gifts upon us. What do we have to give back to God? What obedience can we offer that is commensurate?

The child is a pauper, and so are we. But the child can respond with a smile, a squeal of delight, a jumping up and down. That gift costs nothing but means everything.

And we come to God with nothing in our hand. Any monetary offering seems an insult; any good deed we might claim, a banality. We can give only a poor person's gift, but that means everything to God. We can tell Him "Thank You, Father" and be content to receive without deserving and without returning. We can give our hearts to Him just as much as we can give ourselves to someone on earth whom we love.

I think the only obedience that matters with God is the obedience of poverty. Sometimes in this world poor people or poor countries that receive a handout feel humiliated by the largesse and so harbor ill will against the benefactor. That's why the United States, the most generous nation in history, often finds itself disliked abroad.

But the obedience of grace is a grateful obedience. It's spontaneous and as natural as a baby's giggle.

Seems to me, we come into this world very close to the kingdom of heaven. The Lord deposits us on its threshold, but as we grow up we get messed up. We forget how to give and how to receive. We become shrewd, calculating, conniving. We keep a score of wrongs, harbor grudges. Even in the church, even as preachers, we talk about the kingdom of heaven but live as though the kingdom of this world is all that matters.

Jesus pulls us up short. You need to go back, He tells us, and become like kids again. Ready to receive without deserving. Ready to give without strings. Ready to forgive and forget.

And the really good news is that Jesus tells us how. We can be born again, make a new start, go back to square one (John 3:3-15). He who proclaims the way back also makes it possible.

Chapter Seven

... And From Grandkids

I HAVE TO CONFESS IT: MY grandchildren turn me into a lump of gelatin. After years of patiently enduring friends going gaga over snapshots of their little varmints, I'm outgagaing them all.

Well, Noelene and I waited long enough to lose our heads. After our son married we figured the Johnsson clan would probably show an increase soon, and we waited for signals and signs. And waited. And waited.

As the years passed we muttered to each other that if our kids were going to wait *this* long, they'd have to put up with the consequences. Forget about doting grandparents—we'd be cranky old people who would be no help to them whatever. Let them handle the brats themselves. We even joked about having another child ourselves and handing it off to them to rear.

Then came a baby girl, Madeleine. Let me show you a picture of her, my friend, and if you don't agree that she's as cute as a cat's whisker and the prettiest bundle of love that ever walked the planet, you need to visit an eye doctor fast.

Just one cloud in the perfect picture: Madi was born in Singapore, which is a mighty long way from Washington, D.C. For several months we had to be content with imagining what she was like by means of telephone calls, e-mails, letters, and packages of photographs.

Noelene got to see her first. When she called home to the States, I wanted to know right off the bat, "What's she like?"

"She's gorgeous!"

"But what's she like? Describe her to me."

"Bill, she's gorgeous."

"OK, but tell me more. She's gorgeous, but whom does she look like?"

"All I can say is—she's gorgeous!"

They came home for Christmas, and I saw Madi for myself. I cradled her in my arms and struggled to find words. "She's gorgeous," I finally exclaimed.

Six months later, and they were home again. We all went to the beach. Each morning Madi and I went through a ritual—a long walk on the road that runs by the ocean. Riding in a pack high on my back, she ventured out into the new day like Alice in Wonderland with her chauffeur.

The mile-long stretch going up the beach took plenty of time, if we'd been concerned about the time (which we weren't). Every time I felt her stretching round on my back, I knew she wanted me to stop while she examined a leaf, a tree, a flower, or a pinecone. She wanted to touch them, running little fingers slowly over them, drinking in the texture as she looked away. A bird or dog that came into view brought loud exclamations and flailing of little arms.

Heading back was always faster. Long before we reached the beach house her head had fallen on my shoulder. I gently set the pack down and carried her, limp as a rag doll, up the stairs, a pinecone or shell or other treasure still clutched in her tiny hand.

Noelene and I received a double portion. Nineteen months after Madi's birth, a little sister, Jacqueline, joined her. Born on Easter Sunday, she's a cuddly comedian who stops talking only when she falls asleep. Our cup runneth over.

What is it that makes grandparenting so magical?

Maybe it's the opportunity of parenting without pain—to

relive your own child-rearing years devoid of the hassles and worries that accompanied them. When Terry and Julie were little children, they must have showed all the delight at the world that we now see in Madi and Jackie, but Noelene and I were so concerned with protecting them that we missed out on some wonderful teaching that our kids could have brought us.

Like a sense of wonder. Like the joy of simply being alive. Like the feel of a pinecone.

Yes, the world is monstrous, but grandkids teach us that it's wonderful before it's dangerous. They remind us that the God who made this wonderland has to be infinite in goodness, beauty, and love.

Grandparenting shows that we needn't be so uptight with each other. We can relax and enjoy others simply for themselves. We can take a deep, deep breath and drink in the atmosphere of God's grace.

Noelene and I spoil our grandkids rotten. Are you surprised? I'm beginning to think that our Father God, who is profligate with His gifts, treats us more like a grandparent.

Grace is wasteful, inefficient, scandalous in its lack of discipline. I see that better now. Grace is never irresponsible, but it's generous to the point of recklessness.

Thank you, Madi and Jackie, for bringing so much joy into our lives. And for giving us insights into our own selves—even painful insights—and into God.

And by the way, you who are still in waiting and resolved never to go gaga, be patient. Remember the oft-repeated saying of Scripture that when you're tempted to think your kids will never see the light and do the right thing: "And it came to pass."

Chapter Eight

BREATHING IN GRACE

YOU DON'T HAVE TO CROSS the seas to find grace. You don't have to retreat into a monastery, take a seminar, earn a degree in theology, or look deep within yourself. All you have to do is open your eyes and see. Grace was there—is there—all along.

That's what happened to M. Scott Peck, writer of *The Road Less Traveled*, the hugely successful reflection on his counseling sessions with clients. During the course of the years, as he helped troubled and broken people put their lives together, Peck gradually came to realize that more than his skill was helping make his clients whole. He began to see that the odds in life are stacked in our favor rather than against us, that the universe is upbeat instead of neutral or downbeat, that men and women get well who ought to die, that despite the misery and pain we all experience, joy is real and possible.

By the end of *The Road Less Traveled* Peck finds himself struggling to express what he has found in his work. He isn't a Christian—yet—but he feels compelled to call upon the most Christian word in the vocabulary. Peck begins to talk about grace to describe the miracle he discovered. And erelong that discovery won his heart. His later books reveal that Peck has embraced Jesus as Saviour and Lord.

A recent book every bit as enthralling is Frank McCourt's odyssey about growing up in New York and Dublin, *Angela's Ashes.* Irish, Catholic, and desperately poor, the family struggled with an alcoholic husband and father who couldn't keep a job and drank away the pittance doled out by the government. With its account of the struggle to find food, picking up scraps of coal from the side of the road, the parade of funerals as siblings succumbed to the cold and lack of nourishment, and the shaming by school-masters, welfare authorities, and church—the poor had no advo-cates—the book piles harrowing detail upon harrowing detail.

But McCourt survived. Somehow he survived. Somehow he made his way in the world, broke out of the cycle of poverty, became a highly regarded teacher and now the author of a run-away best-seller (3 million copies sold, translations racing toward 20 languages, a motion picture in production). How did he do it? Or was there help from outside? Yes, help from outside, although unfortunately McCourt hasn't opened his eyes to see it. Grace.

Grace, says Ellen White, is like the atmosphere (see *Steps to Christ*, p. 68). We live in it; it surrounds us; we live because of it. Take away the atmosphere from Planet Earth, and all life will cease. Take away grace from this world, and life will cease just as surely. Even in the saddest situations, even in the cruelest cir-cumstances, the atmosphere surrounds us. Breathe it in, rejoice in it. It will do you good.

One of the strangest but most beautiful books I ever came across was Oliver Sachs' *The Man Who Mistook His Wife for a Hat.* The title, which is no joke, is taken from one of Dr. Sachs' case studies. He has given his life to treating people with rare disorders, people whose brain circuits make wild connections and disorient them in startling ways. Sachs parades before us a procession of men and women marked by radical contrasts—inability to function in the "normal" world but possessing dazzling brilliance of intellect. He introduces us to a pair of identical twins, for instance, who can-not converse with us, but who communicate between themselves in a convoluted number code that "normal" people could not access except by means of a high-powered computer.

As much as Sachs' characters amazed me, his own compassion impressed me even more. Sachs writes with a tender regard and respect for his patients. He sees them as people, not freaks. He refuses to put them out of his thinking and into a mental limbo. He seeks to understand them, to enter their world.

Another of Sachs' case studies has been made into a motion picture. *At First Sight* tells the story of a young man who went totally blind in his second year of life. After learning to cope in the world of the unsighted, he was given the chance to see again through the miracle of modern surgical techniques. In 200 years only eight people had had their sight restored, and he joined the ranks. The sudden return of the light plunged him into a new and alien world for which he was totally unprepared. How he adjusted to his new circumstances—and to the subsequent heartbreak of losing all vision again—makes a poignant tale.

Sachs is a man of grace. His work shows us that even in the bizarre, tragicomic world of the people he treats, we find flashes of light, startling insights and abilities that the rest of us can scarcely fathom. Grace has invaded this land also.

In the Old Testament we read a sad story about a wife driven from home with her son. It wasn't Abraham's finest hour, and certainly not Sarah's, when she, jealous and angry that her servant girl had given birth to the child she couldn't give Abraham, cast her out. So Hagar wandered off into the desert, walked and walked and came to nowhere. It was hot and dry, and she drained the last water from the waterskin. Then Ishmael began to complain. Abandoned and hopeless, she left him in the shade of a bush and waited for him to die.

But Ishmael didn't die. In that desolate place God was there; grace was there. An angel called to Hagar, led her to a spring, saved Ishmael's and her life, and gave her a new start.

We cannot flee from God; we cannot flee from grace. Grace is always there, as close as our nose.

I sat in the university cafeteria at Loma Linda and listened to my longtime friend Paul Landa talk about grace. Paul had just come from treatment at the medical center and had telephoned me that he felt well enough to keep the luncheon appointment we'd made days earlier.

"Exactly one year ago I came for a checkup here at Loma Linda," he told me. "After running all the tests they gave me the news: 'Go home and set your things in order. You will not live to see the Fourth of July.'

"I was devastated, totally unprepared. I was feeling fine—running two miles a day, planning a trek in Nepal. For about a week I couldn't eat or sleep, but then I determined not to lie down and die—literally. I would fight this thing. I had a rare form of cancer and didn't know much about it, but I decided to see what I could find on the Internet."

Paul's research pointed to the National Institutes of Health in Bethesda, Maryland, and experimental treatment. He contacted the NIH and eventually was admitted into their program. And that in turn pointed to a long, difficult, high-risk surgical procedure. Paul decided to take it—his one chance for life.

But grace was there already. "Let me tell you what it felt like as I went into that surgery," he told me. "Hundreds of people—students, colleagues, friends—had told me they were praying for me, and it felt as if there were hundreds of hands under the gurney bearing me along—as if I were floating. I went into surgery without any fear, not knowing if I would come out of it alive, but perfectly at peace."

Paul and I go back a long way, right back to college days at Avondale. For many years I'd respected the power of his intellect and his brilliance in teaching and research. (He taught church history at La Sierra University.) But now as I listened to him that afternoon, I heard a new voice. Paul had been through the fire and had emerged alive. He'd discovered with another Paul that "my grace is sufficient for thee. . . . My strength is made perfect in weakness" (2 Cor. 12:9).

I wish I could tell you that the National Institutes of Health licked Paul's cancer. They couldn't. He kept going back until they told him there was no more point. They extended his life by some 18 months, but at last he succumbed, just before Thanksgiving 1997.

Paul's death was a loss but not a defeat. It was a victory in the face of death, a triumph of faith and hope over death. Just as Jesus' death was.

Paul breathed grace to the last. And so may we.

Chapter Nine

GRACE IN THE FAMILY

HERE'S A NICKEL QUIZ FOR YOU.

1. How many babies in America are born into single-parent homes?

      a. 25 percent

      b. 35 percent

      c. 50 percent

2. Most teenage girls who get pregnant do so between the hours of

      a. 3:00 and 6:00 p.m.

      b. 6:00 p.m. and midnight

      c. after midnight

3. Most teenage crimes are committed between the hours of

      a. 3:00 and 8:00 p.m.

      b. 8:00 p.m. and midnight

      c. after midnight

4. By the time children turn 18, they will have spent 12,000 hours in school but watched television for

      a. 15,000 hours

      b. 20,000 hours

      c. 22,000 hours

5. How many hours do kids today spend each week with their parents?

    a. 15
    b. 25
    c. 30

And here are the answers: c, a, a, c, a. In every case, the worst option of the three presented is the actual one.

The statistic that startled me the most is the one in the second question: teenage girls get pregnant *in the afternoon*. And furthermore, *in their own homes!*

How can this possibly be? The reason is simple: the girls are home alone. No adult is there for them, to give guidance or to provide a role model.

The third question presents a parallel situation. Half of teen crimes happen after school, not late at night. Unsupervised kids are roaming the neighborhood.

You don't have to be a social scientist to know that the American family is in deep, deep trouble. Young people—mere children, actually—are testing the legal code. Boys are getting assault weapons and gunning down teachers and fellow students.

My wife, Noelene, has given her life in ministry to children. I've often heard her say that we live in an age that's unfriendly to kids, and I believe she's correct. Just look at the numbers.

In these United States, every 24 hours:

    3 children die from abuse or neglect.

    6 children commit suicide (if you extend the age parameters to age 24, the figure rises to 13).

Yes, every 24 hours:

    16 youth and young adults are killed by firearms.

    316 are arrested for violent crime.

    403 are arrested for drug use.

And every 24 hours:

    11,420 children are born to teen mothers.

    3,356 drop out of high school.

    5,702 are arrested.

Yes, every 24 hours:

    8,523 are reported abused and neglected.

100,000 are homeless.

14.7 million live in poverty.

These statistics represent babies and little children and boys and girls and teenagers. Behind these numbers lie pain, suffering, loneliness, search for identity, a craving for love.

I wish I could tell you that the tide has turned, that the American family is on the upswing. But I cannot. More and more kids are using drugs, having sex, and becoming involved in other dangerous behaviors at earlier and earlier ages.

The highest-risk kids come from single-parent homes, are kids whose parents don't take an active role in their lives, are economically disadvantaged kids, or are kids who aren't supervised.

So much for society in general, but what about Christians? And what about the Adventist family?

The news isn't good. Adventist kids aren't involved to the same extent, but the pattern of drugs, sex, and dangerous behaviors puts them at risk also. Because we're in the world, the downward trend of society inevitably impacts us. Compounding the problem for many Adventist youth is the fact that 50 to 60 percent don't have the benefit of an Adventist education.

Faced with the threat of growing dangerous behaviors among Adventist kids, the church has tried to respond by giving our young people more information, and giving it to them earlier. We increased the amount of drug and sex education in schools, teaching kids about AIDS, STDs (sexually transmitted diseases), teen pregnancy, and so on. We brought in specialists to warn the kids about the dangers of drugs. We've produced and shown videos and prepared magazines and other materials.

Despite all these efforts, more of our young people are using drugs and having sex than ever before.

We need a new approach, something radically different. The information route is the route that the United States government has taken in its efforts, but it hasn't worked. Some time back President Bill Clinton announced an ad blitz that attempted to shock kids into an awareness of the dangers of drugs. The government enlisted the help of the best ad agencies in the country. The total cost of the campaign was between $2 and 3 billion. I wish the authorities well, but I'm skeptical. It's just more of the same, which has a track record of failure.

I'm not a sociologist or an expert on the family. I'm a concerned parent and grandparent, and I commend the ancient wisdom of the Scriptures, which is as fresh today as back then because it comes from God.

Why not turn to the world's most powerful force for change in human behavior? I mean grace.

Ellen White said it long ago, and she said it right: "The grace of Christ, and this alone, can make this institution [the family] what God designed it should be—an agent for the blessing and uplifting of humanity. And thus the families of earth, in their unity and peace and love, may represent the family of heaven" *(Thoughts From the Mount of Blessing, p. 65).*

In Ephesians 5:21-6:4 we find just how grace can transform our families. Part of the passage is often quoted in the marriage ceremony, but every verse is packed with significance for the Christian family. Let's take a closer look.

First, notice the setting. Paul's letter to the Ephesians contains six chapters, and his message falls neatly into two sections. In the first three chapters Paul sets out the wonder of Jesus Christ, who is God's hidden wisdom manifested in the flesh, the one who has brought us salvation and who reigns as Lord of the church, in which Gentiles now join with the Jews on an equal footing.

At the heart of this message we find grace: "For it is by grace you have been saved, through faith—and this not from yourselves, it is the gift of God—not by works, so that no one can boast. For we are God's workmanship, created in Christ Jesus to do good works, which God prepared in advance for us to do" (Eph. 2:8-10, NIV).

In the second half of Paul's letter, chapters 4-6, he shows how grace works itself out in the life of believers. Again and again his reasoning is: Just as Christ did this for you, so by His grace you are to do the same for others.

"As a prisoner for the Lord, then, I urge you to live a life worthy of the calling you have received," he begins (Eph. 4:1, NIV). "Be kind and compassionate to one another, forgiving each other, *just as in Christ God forgave you,*" he admonishes (verse 32, NIV). "Be imitators of God, therefore, as dearly loved children and live a life of love, *just as Christ loved us and gave himself up for us as a fragrant offering and sacrifice to God,*" he continues (Eph. 5:1, 2, NIV).

Grace, then, isn't something merely for sermons and songs. God intends that grace will permeate every aspect of our being, transform every relationship, make us Christlike in the totality of our lives.

Paul is about to zero in on the family, but before he does so he pauses for a glance at the society of his day. Although the family had been the bastion of Roman society, it had become fearfully degraded. The emperors and their spouses led lives of wanton profligacy, frequenting the brothels and engaging in all manner of sexual practices and perversions.

"But among you there must not be even a hint of sexual immorality, or of any kind of impurity, or of greed, because these are improper for God's holy people," writes Paul (verse 3, NIV). "Have nothing to do with the fruitless deeds of darkness, but rather expose them. For it is shameful even to mention what the disobedient do in secret" (verses 3, 11, 12, NIV).

Now Paul comes to the family. He will speak first about relationships between wives and husbands and then address parent-child relationships. But as the banner over his whole discussion, he immediately states: *"Submit to one another out of reverence for Christ"* (verse 21, NIV).

This principle sets forth a radical new approach to the family. No longer are we hung up about who's the boss. Instead of authority, the essence is servanthood. We aim to serve, not to command; to help, not to rule; to affirm, not to dominate. We're followers of the One who told His disciples: "Whoever wants to become great among you must be your servant, and whoever wants to be first must be your slave—just as the Son of Man did not come to be served, but to serve, and to give his life as a ransom for many" (Matt. 20:26-28, NIV).

We saw what grace is like earlier in this book: grace gives, and grace forgives. Grace *is* Jesus, the one who keeps on giving without conditions, without strings, and who forgives us freely, again and again, lifting us up from our guilt and shame, patting us on the back, and sending us on our way with a new start.

Grace is all that love is—and much more. In our day "love" has become a mushy word used in so many different contexts and with so much emotional and sexual coloration that it lacks specificity. But grace is *love in power, love focused and active, love serving, love giving and forgiving, love transforming the giver and the receiver.*

I think of the way Christians try to run their homes, bring up their children. I think of the way Noelene and I established our home and raised our family. I look around and think back, and the words that ring in my mind are love (of course), respect, authority, obedience, reward, and punishment.

But not much of grace. Oh, grace was there, but not as the central, ruling principle. We weren't constantly acting out how Christ dealt, and deals, with us—certainly I was not. We often were too conscious of having a "good" a "correct" family because I was a pastor, Noelene a minister's wife, and Terry and Julie the children of a preacher. Noelene and I stayed faithful to each other, and our kids behaved well.

We had a happy family, but I wish I had the opportunity to do it over. I'd want to try a different tack. I'd like to serve more, instead of being so concerned about my own needs. I'd be more generous so that the kids would have a better idea how incredibly generous God is. I'd want to throw out forever the crazy self-centered feelings and words over who should be the first to say "I'm sorry" after a tiff. I'd try to help Terry and Julie know clearly—not a shadow of a doubt—that they can never do anything, go anywhere, that would lessen Noelene's and my love for them, that the welcome mat is always out, day and night. And that we're proud of them, and always will be.

Methinks our kids—Adventist kids, Christian kids—have a difficult time grasping the plan of salvation because what we try to teach them after age 10 is out of sync with the way we brought them up. While they're babies, toddlers, and little ones we teach them reward and punishment (disapproval). Then suddenly they're supposed to learn that God deals with us on just the opposite basis, that He doesn't save us because we're good or punish us or turn from us when we're bad.

I've yet to find a child-rearing program that takes seriously the grace principle. I see various well-meaning Christian books and ideas based on a chain of command, authority structures, discipline, leadership, and so on. In light of grace and Paul's counsel in Ephesians 5:21-6:4, I think they miss the mark—some of them woefully so.

Back to Paul. After stating the ruling principle of mutual submission, he summarizes how wives should relate to their husbands. He makes three statements, and in each one he grounds the wife's behavior in her relationship to Jesus Christ. "Wives, submit to your husbands *as to the Lord.* For the husband is the head of the wife *as Christ is the head of the church,* his body, of which he is the Savior. Now *as the church submits to Christ,* so also wives should submit to their husbands in everything" (verses 22-24, NIV).

Does this mean that the husband wears the pants? Not at all. Paul has already laid down the principle of mutual submission, and he is about to show how the husband is to submit to the wife.

The Southern Baptists blew it. Meeting in Salt Lake City for their annual convention on June 9, 1998, they voted a statement on the family, which included that "a wife is to submit graciously to the servant headship of her husband even as the church willingly submits to the leadership of Christ." They voted down the alternative statement—"both husband and wife are to submit graciously to each other"—even though it's an almost direct quote of Ephesians 5:21!

Conclusion: the Southern Baptists, for all their talk about grace, have yet to make grace the ruling principle of the family.

In Ephesians 5:25-32 Paul elaborates the husband's relationship of submission to the wife. Once again Christ provides the model and the motivation: "Husbands, love your wives, *just as Christ loved the church and gave himself up for her. . . . In this same way,* husbands ought to love their wives as their own bodies. . . . After all, no one ever hated his own body, but he feeds and cares for it, *just as Christ does the church*" (NIV).

In verse 33, as Paul concludes his discussion of husband–wife relationships, he returns to the principle of mutual submission that he laid down in verse 21: "However, each one of you also must love his wife as he loves himself, and the wife must respect her husband" (NIV). For Paul, then, the grace-centered family acknowledges the differing roles of wife and husband, but its guiding light is this: Each seeks to serve the other, to defer to the other, just as Christ lived and gave Himself for us.

This is radical stuff. It can begin to work only when the power of grace overflows each heart, rooting out self and transforming us into Jesus' likeness. When we're like Jesus, we'll act like Jesus.

A story making the rounds on the Internet tells about a woman making a purchase in the shopping mall. As she opened her bag to get out the credit card, a TV remote fell out onto the counter. Seeing the startled look in the clerk's eyes, she said, "I asked my husband to come to the mall with me, but he didn't want to. I begged and begged him, but he wouldn't budge. So I came on my own—and took the remote!"

As humorous as the story is, it reflects the tensions of modern American marriages. Without Christ as the head, self takes center stage. Even in a relationship of deep love, competition— "What's in it for me?" and "getting even"—is never far away. That's why love isn't enough.

Paul concludes his discourse on grace in the family with suggestions about parent–child relationships: "Children, obey your parents in the Lord, for this is right. 'Honor your father and mother'— which is the first commandment with a promise—'that it may go well with you and that you may enjoy long life on the earth.' Fathers, do not exasperate your children; instead, bring them up in the training and instruction of the Lord" (Eph. 6:1-4, NIV).

A home where children honor, respect, and obey their parents—every Christian holds this ideal. But the issue is *why?* Why do the children do what's right? Why do they behave as their parents wish? Why do they speak respectfully to their parents?

They may do so because they're afraid to do otherwise. Afraid of what they'll suffer if they don't. Afraid of what will be withheld. Such isn't "obedience"—it's an external conformity, and its future is strictly limited. When the external restraints and motivations are withdrawn, it collapses like a card house. That's why "good" children from "good" Christian homes often cast off all restraints when they cut the family ties.

Another type of "goodness" arises out of respect for the Christian standards of the home. Children love and respect their parents and grow up as "good" children and "good" adults. They never sow wild oats, never bring disgrace on their parents' good name. But they also know that they're "good" and so feel no need of a Saviour.

The only obedience that counts is the obedience which Paul identifies here: "In the Lord." The only goodness is the goodness that comes by His grace, as we realize our sinfulness, accept Jesus' death as our saving sacrifice, and yield ourselves to His love.

How can we help children find this obedience "in the Lord"? I wish I knew the answer.

Part of the answer surely lies in the modeling we provide as parents. Their concept of God will be shaped more by what we do—how we relate to them and to others—than by what we say.

If we're trustworthy, they'll learn trust and find it easier to trust God, whom they cannot see.

If we're generous, they'll find it easier to accept the incredible gift of salvation.

If we affirm them, they'll find it easier to grasp that God regards them as infinitely precious.

If we forgive them easily, they may be able to accept God's infinite forgiveness.

Contrariwise, we can get in the way. We can manipulate their behavior for our own reputation. We can use them as objects for our praise. We can seem harsh and demanding, quick to punish and slow to forgive. And we can school them in a reward-and-punishment pattern that will stay with them for life and make the Holy Spirit's task much harder.

Raising children—who is sufficient for these things? Somehow, in spite of us, good things happen. Let's never forget that God is great, that His love never stops giving and forgiving, nor His Spirit striving. "'Restrain your voice from weeping and your eyes from tears, for your work will be rewarded,' declares the Lord. 'They will return from the land of the enemy. So there is hope for your future,' declares the Lord. 'Your children will return to their own land'" (Jer. 31:16, 17, NIV).

And now I want to take up a final aspect of grace in the family. The family is the locus not only of our most tender joys but also of our deepest pain. All around North America I find dear people whose hearts are breaking because a loved one—child, spouse, sibling, grandchild—no longer walks with the Lord. I find people tortured with guilt and regret, asking "What did we do wrong?" and blaming themselves for the course the cherished one has taken.

None of us is—or has been—a perfect parent. Despite our keen desires and best efforts, we fall short of what we might be and do. In fact, there was ever only one perfect family—God's. And even in that perfect family something went terribly wrong. First Lucifer, and then a third of the angels, turned their backs on God, rejected His love and overtures, and went their own way.

So let's remember that God does not—nor can we—determine the outcome of an individual's life. We can influence and we can pray, but ultimately the decision rests outside our power. That's the way God set it up, and that's the way it still happens.

But God supplies grace when our hearts are breaking. He never gives up, and He enables us never to give up. He gives grace so that we can keep hoping, praying, loving.

Billy Graham, who preached grace to millions, learned that in his own family. His autobiography, *Just as I Am,* is moving because of the warmth toward people it exudes—here's a person without a grain of bitterness in his bones—and because of its refreshing candor. Graham has lived a life filled with activity, travel, and innovation. He's been the confidant of the world's great and the guest of all United States presidents from Harry Truman on.

In the midst of all this work for the Lord, however, Billy Graham's own family suffered. His children grew up in the shadow of a world celebrity, who was also an absent father. Graham's first-born, his son Ned, became alienated from his father and from God.

Billy doesn't spare himself as he tells the story of his life. He doesn't conveniently leave out this unwelcome chapter, doesn't try to spin the facts. He tells it like it is, lets the bitter facts of his failure hang out for all the world to see.

All of us, no matter what our denominational affiliation, can learn from Graham's honesty. By uncorking our pain, by laying off the cloak of pretense, we can find the healing of heart that God seeks to provide.

I've heard some people say, and I've sometimes felt it within myself, "If my children aren't with me in heaven, then I don't want to be there." But that sentiment reveals a terrible lack in our understanding of grace. With or without our children, with or without our spouse, Jesus will be all we desire when we see Him face to face. He will be all in all.

He can be that right now also, if we let Him.

Chapter Ten

GRACE BOUQUETS

WHEN IT COMES TO SPEECH, this is a graceless age. Polite conversation, once the hallmark of culture, has yielded to that modern barbarism, the talk show.

"Everywhere we turn, there is evidence that, in public discourse, we prize contentiousness and aggression more than cooperation and conciliation," wrote Deborah Tannen, professor of linguistics at Georgetown University, in a Washington *Post* article. Her book *The Argument Culture* was published by Random House.

Tannen describes a meeting with another guest as she was about to go on a television talk show. This man, who wore a shirt and tie and a floor-length skirt, had red hair down to his waist. He told Tannen, "When I get out there, I'm going to attack you. But don't take it personally. That's why they invite me on, so that's what I'm going to do."

And that's what he did. When the show began, Tannen hardly had finished a couple of sentences before the man threw out his hands in a gesture of anger and began to shriek out accusations against her and all women. Then Tannen watched in amazement as the studio audience erupted in vicious attacks on the other women guests.

This is the media age, and the media thrive on confrontation. The goal isn't to share perspectives in a common search for truth, but rather to best your opponents in debate, even if it means interrupting or outshouting them.

Notes Tannen: "Headlines blare about the Star Wars, the Mommy Wars, the Baby Wars, the Mammography Wars; everything is posed in terms of battles and duels, winners and losers, conflicts and disputes. Biographies have metamorphosed into demonographies whose authors don't just portray their subjects warts and all but set out to dig up as much dirt as possible, as if the story of a person's life is contained in the warts, only the warts, and nothing but the warts" ("For Argument's Sake," Washington *Post,* Mar. 15, 1998).

Inevitably, the spirit of the age impacts the church. You'd be shocked at mail that occasionally comes across my desk. Some time ago, for instance, I received a letter that consisted of a page torn out of the *Review* with words scrawled across it, including an obscenity in large letters. And the writer signed himself a "sixth-generation Adventist"!

I've attended Sabbath school classes whose stated purpose is "to have a good discussion"—regardless of whether or not the dialogue deals with the lesson or leaves members spiritually uplifted. Now, I love a good discussion and encourage it, but discussion isn't an end in itself. Jesus alone and His glory must be our goal in all we do, or we fall into a worldly mode of operation.

And, of course, we easily slip into harshness and criticism, faultfinding and gossip. That again is the spirit of the age injecting itself. This is the day of the analyst and the expert seated in the air-conditioned booth far above the action, second-guessing with superior wisdom the coach, umpire, and players.

One morning I was making the rounds of the *Adventist Review* offices, just dropping by to say hello. I met managing editor Myrna Tetz, looking not quite her usual perky self. We paused to talk about a letter she'd received in response to the special issue "People of Hope," which she'd worked on.

We customarily prepare four undated specials each year, and I assign one editor to carry the main load for each issue. Because Myrna has a burden for Adventists to break out of their cocoons and make contact with their friends and neighbors, she was the obvious choice to spearhead efforts on this issue intended for church members to give to their acquaintances. Myrna threw herself into the project, enlisting the help of the staff of the General Conference Communication Department and seeking to make it a banner issue. And it was—a 64-page magazine that put Adventism's best foot forward.

Many people liked the issue and let her know that her months of planning and work had paid off. But in the publishing business you never please everyone, and Myrna had just read a letter that deflated her. It listed all the things "wrong" with the issue and then included a comment that the copies bought by the writer's local church maybe should be gathered together to make a bonfire!

You can receive 20 letters that applaud your efforts, but the single one which sticks in your craw is the one that lashes out at you.

Still shaking my head over the sour letter that ruined Myrna's morning, I stopped by Andy Nash's office. He seemed a bit subdued, so I stayed to chat awhile. We got onto Friday Hope, a monthly meeting held right at General Conference headquarters targeting the young adults employed in the complex and their peers in the Washington, D.C., area. Andy got the idea and recruited friends to help. They put out flyers, formed a musical group, arranged speakers, organized video clips, prepared refreshments. They stayed up nights after work to practice music and rehearse skits.

And it worked. About 200 young people showed up to worship and fellowship. At Andy's urging, Noelene and I attended also—feeling a bit like gate-crashers, but soon we were made to feel welcome. It was an evening that glorified the Lord.

But not everyone thought so. Just before I dropped in on Andy that morning, someone had come by and observed that Friday Hope was "a lot of fluff." I could tell that person had hurt Andy.

Destructive criticism is always bad, but when it's directed at young persons who have done their level best to do something good, it's evil. If we can't find a word of commendation for our young people's efforts, let's keep our lips buttoned.

"Do not let any unwholesome talk come out of your mouths, but only what is helpful for building others up according to their needs, that it may benefit those who listen," wrote the apostle Paul (Eph. 4:29, NIV). The word translated "unwholesome" is the Greek *sapros*, which really has a stronger meaning—"decayed" or "rotten." In Greek literature it was used of spoiled fish, so Paul is saying: "Don't let your talk stink like rotten fish!"

We humans at the dawn of the new millennium are stinking up the planet. We've invented shows to tear people apart and shows to make people laugh. We've taken God's gift of mirth and perverted it into canned guffaws and the drivel of stand-up comedians.

Listen again to Paul: "Nor should there be any obscenity, foolish talk or coarse joking, which are out of place, but rather thanksgiving" (Eph. 5:4, NIV).

Instead of talk that stinks like rotten fish, how much better are words that come like grace bouquets. Instead of waiting until the funeral to say it with flowers, why not let the living get the benefit?

As a people who profess God's name in these last days, may He give us words that heal instead of wound, that build up instead of tear down, that encourage and inspire—grace words. May our speech be like Jesus', seasoned with salt.

As I look back over my life, so many *sapros* words come to mind. I regret my smart-aleck comments that made others laugh but wounded a heart; the proud, boastful, self-serving talk; the foolish and careless remark; the bullying, threatening innuendo. James was right: "If anyone is never at fault in what he says, he is a perfect man, able to keep his whole body in check" (James 3:2, NIV). And I'm not a perfect man.

Nevertheless, delightful surprises keep coming up out of the past. Someone reminds me of something I said in a sermon many years ago. I can't even remember the sermon or the occasion, but the Lord somehow used this far-from-perfect preacher to toss a grace bouquet in someone's direction.

A young man meets me and repeats verbatim my words spoken privately to him one night. I'd preached for the evening service at camp meeting, and he waited in line after the meeting and then asked my counsel on an item of great importance to him. I was tired, but the Lord gave me a word in due season for the young seeker.

Then, of course, there's the ongoing response through letters to the words I've written . . . and that's another and beautiful story of its own.

Let's hear it from Paul one more time: "Be gracious in your speech. The goal is to bring out the best in others in a conversation, not put them down, not cut them out" (Col. 4:6, Message). I love this paraphrase; it gets to the nub of Christian conversation.

Noelene and I have conducted several seminars for women on how to participate in committees. We got into this arena by chance—someone in the General Conference thought we could do it and asked us. After that, others heard about it, and the invitations began to come in. The Adventist Church runs on committees, but women up to now have largely been shut out of them. I present the nuts-and-bolts stuff about calling the question, tabling a motion, etc., but Noelene does the real thing—how to act when you're the token woman, when the male members assume you'll automatically sit quiet as a mouse and of course handle the secretarial chores. Methinks men need this seminar also, if we all as Christians will seek to bring out the best in others in conversation, not put them down, and not cut them out.

Throughout the years I've been flung grace bouquets by many different people. A teacher as well as a school principal who gave me an encouraging word and confidence that I could strive for the top. My mother, who hardly seemed capable of uttering anything cutting to anyone and especially to me. And a host of others, most of them people I've never met, who keep the stream of love flowing toward this office in little messages of affirmation and the precious information that they keep me and the other staff members constantly in their prayers.

To single out a couple of people for particular mention seems risky and unfair to hundreds, maybe thousands of others—only the Lord knows how many. Think of these that follow as examples, representations of a crowd to which many who read this book belong.

I don't remember when I first met Arnold Wallenkampf. He was one of those people who become so close to you that you feel you've known them all your life. We shared Swedish roots—he was born in that country, as was my father—and a love of Bible study and theology. "Walle" was a big, strapping man with a broad Nordic forehead, bright blue eyes, and a booming laugh. Laughter would take over his body: he'd slap his side, throw back his head, and enjoy the moment with his whole being.

He would come by the office with an ostensible reason but more often than not just to talk. And he always said it with flowers. Not fake, plastic flowers of flattery, but words from the heart, affirming words, encouraging words, grace bouquets. He knew how to give advice without lecturing, how to counsel without any ego intrusion.

After he retired and moved away from the Washington area, he would call me from time to time or occasionally show up unexpectedly at my door. And always he brought a grace bouquet. I miss him keenly.

One day when I called at his retirement home in Virginia, he revealed that it was his eightieth birthday. Of course, that led to the booming laugh. Then I heard his wife, Mae, say in the background, "Tell him the other news." And then, with more laughter, he informed me that—at 80—he'd just become a grandfather for the first time! "We skipped a generation," he said, as he explained how the numbers worked out, interspersed with more laughter.

Another person. "You have the perfect secretary," someone told me once. "She always makes callers feel they're important." Indeed. In Chitra Barnabas the Lord provided someone with the gentlest of spirits and most courteous of manners.

Long ago I came to realize that one can get a pretty fair indication of what the boss is like by the type of receptionist employed. Apart from her other qualities, Chitra is the ideal secretary for me because of her genuine caring for people, whether "famous" or "nobodies." We have a running joke at the *Adventist Review* office that Chitra is a tyrant and everyone is afraid of her—which is our way of complimenting this woman who daily throws grace bouquets.

Just one more. This will be brief—not because there's little to say but so much, and so freighted with the stuff of my life. Through the words of Noelene, wife of my youth and my life's partner and friend, I am refreshed, supported, and strengthened. She's wise and good and ardently devoted to the Lord. Only one question continues to amaze me: How come she so often turns out to be right?

Jesus' searching test—"I tell you, on the day of judgment men will render account for every careless word they utter; for by your words you will be justified, and by your words you will be condemned" (Matt. 12:36, 37, RSV)—seems severe. But the fact is that our words show who we really are. They reveal that the grace of a loving God has touched and changed our hearts and lips, or else, like Peter sitting by the fire while Jesus faced His accusers, that we've not yet yielded to the gracious Pattern.

Those same lips, those lying lips, spoke truth a few months later. Along with John, Peter boldly proclaimed Jesus of Nazareth as the Messiah and the only Saviour of the world. His words amazed the religious leaders of Jerusalem, but then they recalled that he'd been with Jesus (see Acts 4:5-13).

After Pentecost, notes Ellen White, "the language of the disciples was pure, simple, and accurate, whether they spoke in their native tongue or in a foreign language" (*The Acts of the Apostles*, p. 40). That's an ideal for every Christian in this age of talk shows. But grace words come only, as they did for the disciples, as a gift of grace.

Chapter Eleven

CHRISTINE

SEVERAL YEARS AGO NOELENE received a telephone call at the office that should have been directed elsewhere. The woman on the other end was inquiring about an Adventist church that might have a ministry for teens with mental impairment. Noelene's office deals with children's ministries, not teens, but the Lord had a purpose in hooking up Noelene with Brenda Peace that day.

Brenda had recently lost her 20-year-old daughter, Julie, a student at the University of Maryland. She'd been killed outright in a car accident. Mother and daughter were a pair: They looked alike and had the same warm, outgoing personality. Julie would burst through the door, throw herself on Brenda's lap, give her a hug, and say, "I love you, Mom."

Now she'd been snatched away, and life seemed unbearable for Brenda and her husband, Blair. For Brenda the loss came with the sharp edge of guilt. She'd been brought up Adventist but had never experienced grace in its liberating reality. Knowing only the rules, she quit going to church as a teenager. Day by day, as she struggled just to get up and face another morning, her mind ached for Julie and the thought that if she,

Brenda, had stayed in the Adventist Church, God might have spared her daughter.

I first met Brenda and Blair during this period. Both were like zombies, going through the motions but detached from life. Brenda's face bore the marks of extreme grief. She seemed like a person who would never laugh again. Blair had internalized his grief.

The day of that first contact, the misdirected telephone call, Noelene promised that she'd phone around and find out if any church had a ministry for mentally challenged children. She also told Brenda of an Adventist church with a grief recovery program—in fact, the congregation where we have our membership, Sligo, was running one.

Brenda began to attend, began to heal. But the gnawing guilt still bothered her. She and Blair had attended other churches, but Brenda felt she should be back with the Adventists. Sligo didn't appeal to her. With its 3,000-plus membership it didn't fit her idea of church. She was looking for a smaller Adventist church home, but one that could cater to the spiritual needs of the whole family.

The Peaces had another child, a daughter named Christine, born three years after Julie. Christine was big and strong and daddy's girl, but with an IQ of a 5-year-old. During the week she attended a school for kids with special needs. Sabbaths she needed a church that catered to her requirements.

Noelene called around the Washington, D.C., area. Adventist churches abound around here—more than 70 of them—but not one offered a Sabbath school for children with special needs. Brenda and Blair had been attending a large church of another denomination, which provided for Christine, and despite Brenda's strong desire to come back to the Adventist family, she and Blair weren't about to uproot their dear Christine and place her in an environment in which she might be misunderstood and unhappy.

What to do? Noelene got an idea: She'd start a special class just for Christine. Maybe parents of other children like Christine would hear about it and start coming to church also.

It was a beautiful idea that I thought was dead wrong.

"Listen," I told Noelene, "you already have too much on your plate. You're working more than full-time without this. How do you expect to handle the extra load? Besides, you travel a lot, and what will happen to the class when you're out of town?"

I was the one who was dead wrong. Of all the many wonderful acts of ministry I've seen Noelene get involved in, none was more inspired by the Lord than this one. I look back on it now and see the circle of grace that flowed from it—to Christine, who found a welcoming new home; to Brenda and Blair, who found a community that accepted and loved them and where Brenda gradually learned to cease blaming herself for her daughter's death; to Sligo church, which found two unselfish, giving adults who don't just warm the pews but are always there to help, whether it's fellowship dinners, evangelistic meetings, Vacation Bible Schools, or whatever; and to Noelene and me, who found new friends who've become very close. But that's how I see it now; the light dawned slowly for me.

Through Brenda, who was plugged into the network of parents of children with special needs, Noelene learned of an all-day seminar being put on by a Lutheran church in Frederick, Maryland. (The Lutherans seem to have made helping such children a major ministry—the Lord bless them for it.) She and Brenda took off for the day—a Sabbath—leaving me alone and fuming at Noelene's foolishness.

Noelene came home bubbling over with what she'd experienced at the seminar. I was still skeptical, but she convinced me to view a couple of videos she'd picked up. The videos weren't glitzy, expensive productions—just footage of children with special needs interacting with adults. They were intended to provide training for anyone who wished to get involved.

This was a new world to me. Much of my life has been spent in an academic environment, and I feel immediately at home whenever I set foot on a college or university campus anywhere in the world. I simply hadn't come to terms with the world of the mentally challenged. But as I watched the videos something started to happen to me. I saw children, some of them grown to adult size, none of them especially physically attractive and some unattractive, in settings of joy and love. The simplicity of their enjoyment and the purity of their love for Jesus grabbed at my heart.

I watched and slowly, slowly was overwhelmed. From the "normal" people with these kids, such love and affection, such acceptance and affirmation, flowed as I'd never witnessed. "You don't have to be a certain age to be a teacher. You can be a teenager or in your 60s or 70s," intoned the voice-over. "You don't need a college degree or special training. All it takes is the ability to love."

That Saturday evening the Lord gave me a glimpse of grace. I saw grace manifested in the lives and work of those godly men and women who'd given themselves to bring Jesus to these special people. Later, as Noelene and I became closer and closer friends of the Peace family, I would see that manifestation again and again in the tender, understanding way they related to their daughter.

I remember well the first Sabbath we invited them home for Sabbath dinner. By now the light had begun to return to Brenda's eyes, and while not a day passed that she didn't think of Julie, she'd begun to live again. We sat around the dining table, two of us and four of them—Blair, Brenda, Christine, and Brenda's mother, who was visiting from Richmond, Virginia. The mood was a bit stiff—we were still getting acquainted. And the Peaces were apprehensive lest Christine spill her drink or somehow spoil the occasion.

They needn't have worried: I helped them out. In an effort to liven up the conversation, I made a sweeping gesture (I use my hands a lot when I speak at any time), caught the edge of my glass of juice, and transported its contents into the lap of Brenda's mother! I hadn't intended it (obviously), but the faux pas broke the ice. Brenda's mother was a great sport, and the whole family was relieved that whatever else might happen (nothing did), the host himself had lowered the bar to a new depth.

Well, Brenda and Blair attended Sligo regularly and studied the Bible, and Christine went to her special class of one—until one day Noelene was traveling and Christine discovered primary class. Her assigned teacher, a young man, presented her with a green

Bible, and her heart was won. She graduated to primary division, where the kids showed grace their own way. And one Sabbath the congregation witnessed a baptism as Brenda and Christine followed the example of their Lord and Saviour.

A story of life out of death, of grace out of tragedy.

But there's more.

On a Thursday morning before Good Friday the Montgomery County police called my office. I'd gone out on an errand, so the call went through to Noelene. It was Brenda, breaking up so badly that Noelene couldn't get any details beyond the fact that something tragic had happened to Christine.

By the time I got the news and rushed to the Peace home, neighbors were gathering. Noelene had arrived some time earlier. Representatives from the coroner's office in Baltimore were upstairs in Christine's bedroom.

Christine had been on spring break. She and Blair had planned a big day together. He wouldn't go to work; they'd sleep in late, then go out for breakfast. But when Blair went to call her about 9:00 she didn't stir. She'd died in her sleep, presumably suffocating from a seizure.

I stood numb as Blair called the funeral home to make arrangements. Same people, same situation. "Just do it like you did before," he said in a voice that came from far away.

Christine was one month away from her twenty-first birthday.

Two daughters; both gone.

Two daughters; both dead at 20.

What can you say at a time like this? Nothing that says anything. You can only be there, there to hug and to listen and to suffer with hearts overwhelmed by life's cruelty.

Immediately Brenda asked me to conduct the funeral. Noelene and I spent a lot of time in that home of tragedy, especially during the first two days. And thereby I came to see clearly for the first time an aspect of Brenda's life that had been staring me in the face all the time, but I'd been too stupid to see.

The friends who came by the home and later at the viewing

at the funeral home helped take the scales from my eyes. As I met more and more of them—and there were many—I came to realize the common factor: Most were associated through children with special needs. Classmates of Christine. Teachers of Christine. The principal of Christine's school. A Methodist who in retirement heads a foundation to provide homes for children with special needs whose parents are aging.

The quality of these people I met was extraordinary. Their relationship with Brenda and Blair and with one another went way beyond friendship. It was much more than being in the same boat of caring for "difficult" kids. They had a radiance about them, an unselfish love more profound than I had ever encountered in any group.

Gradually they helped me realize—without trying to instruct me—that these "special" children are special in ways I hadn't dreamed of. I learned that kids such as Christine and her "boyfriend" Josh and her friend Gretchen (who told me as soon as I met her that she wanted to speak at Christine's funeral, and did) are blessed with rare and beautiful gifts. I learned that they have the ability to love without hating, that they can experience good without knowing evil, that they can find joy in the simplest amusements.

This, their world, is pure grace.

That Good Friday Noelene and I spent much of the day with Blair and Brenda. The following morning I was slated to preach for the Easter services at Sligo church, but when I went to bed my head was full of Christine and Brenda and Blair. After keeping Noelene awake for a couple of hours, I moved to the guest room, tossed around, but still couldn't drop off. I went downstairs, put on a Mozart CD, threw a blanket over my shoulders, and stretched out on the family room sofa.

But this night even Mozart didn't work for me. Sometime in the wee hours I gave up trying, dressed, and went walking. The night was clear and still, and the air was heavy with the scents of spring blossoms. I was scheduled to preach in but a few hours, but my thoughts were on what I would say on Monday morning when we would bid a last farewell to Christine.

As I walked on and on, a phrase floated through my brain and snagged on something and lodged. The words kept coming back, stronger, louder: "Green was her color." Gradually other ideas attached themselves, and I knew what Monday's message would be.

I walked until the words had all come together. Then I went home, put on Mozart's piano sonata K 15, stretched out on the sofa, and fell asleep.

After a couple of hours I was up and writing.

Green Was Her Color

Green was her color.

Size and shape, fit and cloth didn't matter if the color was right. Christine would be at the Community Services center with Brenda and would go back and haul out a load of outfits. Dresses, jackets, blouses, pairs of shoes—they'd all be green.

"Look at these dresses," Brenda would say. "They're size 10. You need to look for 18s!"

Christine would go back for more. But they were just like the others—size 10s and shoes that didn't fit. Only one thing mattered—they were all green.

Green was her color.

She was born in May when spring was in the full, when the trees wore silken jackets of green, when grass covered the fields and the earth throbbed with life and vitality.

She fell asleep on the first day of April. Winter hung on late this year, but she lived to see the snow melt away, the first buds shoot out, and the greening of the land return.

Green was her color.

Christine was a spring child. She was a child of eternal sweetness and love who could go up to perfect strangers, give them a big hug and say, "I love you." Who could resist this spring child?

She knew love; she never learned evil.

She knew the affection and protection of parents. She knew the warmth of friends such as Gretchen and Josh. She knew the joy of her dog, Freckles. She knew the taste of food, especially nachos. She knew fun. She knew contentment, happy to play with her Lego brand building set for hours. She knew love. She knew the love of Jesus.

She never learned evil. She was shielded from the crookedness and ugliness, the deceit and cruelty that most of us know, that lie so close at hand and suck us into their orbits.

So who can say who was disabled? Was it the spring child, or was it we who think we are whole? The spring child left behind a legacy of pure sweetness and unconditional love, a legacy of good.

In this church we take as our motto "All are gifted; all are valued." No doubt some people looked at Christine and asked themselves How is this girl gifted? But we here today, who have looked through the open gates of heaven, know that gifted she was, gifted with a rare and precious ability that any church would desire to find among its members.

Green was her color.

Jesus told many parables about the spring. In one of them He said, "The kingdom of heaven is like a man who sowed good seed in his field. But while everyone was sleeping, his enemy came and sowed weeds among the wheat, and went away. When the wheat sprouted and formed heads [when the color green appeared], then the weeds also appeared.

"The owner's servants came to him and said, 'Sir, didn't you sow good seed in your field? Where then did the weeds come from?'

"'An enemy did this,' he replied" (Matt. 13:24-28, NIV).

Life is marvelous, and life is monstrous. Blair and Brenda, during the past few days you have racked your brains trying to find out "Why? Why, God? Why?" Been there—done that! You went through all this three and a half years ago. How could God put you through it again?

An enemy has done this. God isn't the author of this tragedy; neither are you the cause. Nothing you have done or failed to do has been a factor in the loss of your beloved daughter.

An enemy has done this.

Although God isn't the author of evil, He can turn even evil to a good purpose. The passing of His saints such as Christine causes the rest of us who live on to reflect on who we are and what sort of legacy we will leave when our name is called. And thus, even through her leaving us, Christine continues to bring the greening.

Green was her color.

Her favorite song was "Jesus loves me, this I know, for the Bible tells me so."

She knew love. She knew that Jesus loved her. All that matters in religion comes down to that. All that matters in life comes down to that.

Jesus, too, was a spring child. In the spring of the year, when the Passover moon was at the full and the Holy Land was covered in green, He went to the cross.

"There is a green hill far away,
Without a city wall,
Where the dear Lord was crucified,
Who died to save us all" (Cecil Francis Alexander).

By His dying He gave life to all. With His stripes we all—Christine included—are healed.

Green was her color.

Because He lives, we too shall live. "I am the Living One," He says. "I was dead, and behold I am alive for ever and ever! And I hold the keys of death and Hades" (Rev. 1:18, NIV). "I am the resurrection and the life. [She] who believes in me will live, even though [she] dies" (John 11:25, NIV).

The greening is coming. It is coming as surely as spring came at last this year.

The greening when the desert shall bloom like the rose and the earth give up the dead. When God will dwell with His people and wipe away every tear. When we shall be free from heartache and loss and suffering. When Christine will be with us forever.

No dark valleys then. No death valleys. There will be a new heaven and a new earth, for the first heaven and the first earth will have passed away.

Christine will be so happy in that day.

Green was her color, and green will be her color.

Chapter Twelve

VACATION FROM HELL

ONE DAY WHEN I WAS TELLING Noelene about ideas for this book she asked, "Will you have a chapter on our vacation in south India?"

I looked at her aghast. We'd taken several trips to the south, but one turned out so bad that I'd blocked it from my mind. And that was the one, I knew, she was thinking about.

"No," I replied. "I don't see how *that* vacation fits in a book on grace. It was a vacation from hell."

"Well, have you ever considered how . . . and how . . . and how . . . ?"

Of course I hadn't. But right then I started to, and it all came back but with a new perspective.

India is a hot country. From New Year's on the mercury starts to rise until it hits 100°F in March. Still it climbs. If you go out in the midday sun, along with mad dogs and Englishmen, the sun burns a hole through the shirt on your back. The air shimmers, and you join Shadrach, Meshach, and Abednego. Higher and higher, hotter and hotter, until the monsoon makes its way from south to north and breaks the inferno. Somehow you have to find a way to make it from the end of March until mid-June, when the clouds and downpours bring relief.

Spicer College doesn't have air-conditioning, so the school year runs from late June to late March. The summer session of four to six weeks, which follows commencement, is purgatory for teacher and student alike.

But way down south beyond the city of Bangalore, at the end of a narrow serpentine access road, missionaries long ago built a hill station. The little town of Kodaikanal, with its 7,000-foot altitude, offered sunny, pleasant days and nights almost cool enough for a wood fire. In the fresh, bracing air color quickly returned to kids' pale cheeks, and energy came surging back.

So by late April and early May you could see staff members packing for the trip south. It was a long haul, and a tough one— 900 miles along narrow roads without shoulders and crowded with suicidal truck drivers, bullock carts, bicycles, and pedestrians.

Our vehicles were all old: The government had stopped imports of new cars after India attained independence in the late 1940s. Parts became more and more scarce, but with great ingenuity local mechanics patched and improvised and kept us on the road.

The cars heading to Kodaikanal were fearfully and wonderfully made—and more fearfully than wonderfully. Because daytime was so blazing hot and we didn't have air-conditioning, we usually drove all night and as far as we could get the next morning until the heat took over. We'd then seek out a *dakbungla,* a government-operated travelers' stop, to rest up during the heat of the day. These facilities were kept reasonably clean and—most important on our limited budget—cost very little.

Our car was maybe the most beat-up vehicle on campus, but we got it cheap. One day the cops showed up, and we learned that the car previously had been used in a moonshine operation. (India had prohibition at that time.) A 1948 Chevy, it had the old divided windshield. The metal used for the door and window handles was of inferior grade—the handles would wind off the gear, and we were forever trying to get the windows up or down or to get out from inside.

Since the car had been built in the United States for export, the steering wheel was on the right-hand side, which was OK for India because they use the British system for driving. But the adaptation in Detroit came via a series of extra linkages between the hand shift on the steering wheel and the gearbox. Each of the links had a ball joint, which was fine when the car was new, but by the time we owned it the joints were worn and the links would stick. We'd have to get out, lift up the bonnet (hood), and jiggle the links loose.

Does it sound like fun yet?

This year, the infamous year, I was apprehensive about the Chevy's ability to get us to Kodaikanal and back. No worries about the engine: The good old straight six never missed a beat. I'll wager it's still powering up something or other. When I had Sam Irani, the local mechanic, check the Chevy, he gave a noncommittal answer rather than the thumbs-up I was hoping for.

But it was terribly hot and the green hills were calling, so we went for broke. We loaded the car with supplies for the trip and in we got—Noelene, our two kids, a friend who'd come to Spicer for the summer school, and me. By the time we hit the road we were jammed solid from the rear seat to the narrow back window.

Several hours into the first day I sensed that the Chevy wasn't handling right. When I tried the brakes, nothing happened. I carefully brought the car to a stop and got out, butterflies in my stomach. The stain on the front left wheel said it all. We'd lost our brake fluid.

To get the picture, you have to realize that we were out in the countryside with no help available. No cell phone. No phones of any sort. No AAA. No tow trucks. And no credit cards. (They hadn't been invented yet.) Not even checks—when we traveled we carried cash for all our needs.

Slowly, using the gears for braking, we made our way to the nearest town, found a mechanic, and looked for a cheap hotel.

Within 24 hours we were on the road again—with a big hole in our cash supply. But at last we motored up the long switchback road to Kodai and, thoroughly worn out, joined our vacationing friends.

I couldn't enjoy the weeks in the hills that year. The trip south had spooked me, and I kept wondering about the journey back.

Soon it was time to set out. One of the missionaries who heard about our problems kindly lent us money so that we could have a cushion of cash for our needs. But I still didn't feel right about the car. When we overnighted later at a friend's home in Bangalore, I put the car into a service station for a complete check.

The following night, sometime in the wee hours, I was driving down the lonely, unlit highway, figuring how long it would take us to reach home if we kept right on. Noelene and the children were fast asleep; no other vehicle was on the road; all I heard was the steady chugging of the faithful old Chevy engine.

Suddenly the hair on my neck stood up. From the driveshaft I detected an ominous, grinding sound. I waited for it to go away; I willed it to cease. But it became louder and turned into a loud horrible clunking that awoke the family. We were in trouble.

Just before the differential box seized up, I saw a little area with two gas pumps and a tiny office. I pulled in and waited for the dawn, wondering what the new day would bring. We were hundreds of miles from home and stuck, with a car that was going nowhere. We had no way of contacting anyone for help. And we were almost broke.

I blamed myself for putting my dear ones in danger. Ever a risk taker, I'd taken one chance too many. I should never have set out from home with the car in the condition it was, and now we were all in a big mess.

When the light came I saw a small, storelike structure across the road. And when I woke up the owner, he turned out to be a young man—with an auto repair business!

He was soon under the Chevy. Before long he had the differential out and confirmed our fears—it was shot. And we learned why—no oil. Whoever had checked out our car in Bangalore had either left off the oil cap or failed to tighten it, because it was gone and with it all the differential oil.

Problem: Where do you find a replacement differential gearbox for a 1948 Chevy out in the sticks of India? (Which will be followed by a second question, even weightier if you solve that one.)

Answer: Anything is possible in India. The country is full of resourceful people who find a way.

In our case the way led to *chor bazaar,* the thieves' market. My new friend and I hopped on a bus and rode into the nearest town, searching through the *chor bazaar* until we found one—a 1948 Chevy differential, not new, but in good condition.

Now came the second problem. You guessed it—I didn't have the do-re-mi to pay for the differential.

I cast myself on the kindness of the seller, telling him about our plight, giving him the little cash I had left and promising to send him a money order for the balance when we got back to Pune. The guy looked at me hard—what sort of *sahib* was this? He listened to the pleas of my young friend and gave us the differential.

We took a bus back to Noelene and the kids. For hours the young guy was under the Chevy, trying to get the new differential fitted. The shadows were getting long when at last he gave us the word, and we loaded the car. I thanked him as profusely as my limited Hindi allowed, took his name and address for mailing the money order, and feeling almost lighthearted, set out for home. With a clear run we would pull onto the campus of Spicer College the next morning.

My mind and my eyes were on the road, and I hardly heard what Noelene said as we drove off. "What's up with that young fellow? He ran away as if he's scared of something!"

At last, a night without trauma. A night with the straight six chugging and the driveshaft giving a steady, reassuring whir. Noelene and the kids were sound asleep, and it was late, late. We'd just passed the town of Kolhapur and had only three or four hours to go.

Sudden I heard a clunk and a bump, and we stopped at the edge of the road with the left side of the car tilted down. I hopped out of the car and noticed that the left wheel was off. I was shivering from weariness and worry.

Almost immediately bright lights were bearing down on us. A big rig had stopped, and the driver was walking over. He sized up the situation and explained the problem. At the last stop the young mechanic had fitted the wheel lugs wrong side in, and they gradually wore through the rim. This car was going no farther that night.

The driver offered to give us a ride. But where to? I remembered that we had a national worker in Kolhapur, vaguely recalling the area where he lived. The driver seemed to understand. He hauled up Terry and Julie into the high cab, and Noelene and I climbed aboard, grabbing a few clothes from the car (which wouldn't lock), and we set out. Then Pastor Shinde was waking up and taking us in at an ungodly hour, and we were falling asleep.

The next day he phoned Pastor Ellsworth Hetke, the mission president for the area, and soon we were at the Hetkes, and our car was being fixed. And although we left most of our stuff in the unlocked car, and although the place where we broke down was close by the *chor bazaar*, not one thing had been taken.

As I write these words, it's like living through a bad dream for the second time. It was a vacation from hell.

But what did the psalmist say? "If I make my bed in hell, behold, thou art there" (Ps. 139:8).

Noelene was right: Grace was there.

I look back and think of the "coincidences." Breaking down on the lonely road at the one place where someone had enough mechanical skill to provide a measure of help. The hard-bitten merchant of the *chor bazaar*, who put his money on the longest of shots. The truck driver who just happened to arrive when I was at the point of desperation.

Is God good? All the time.

Even when we think we're in hell.

Chapter Thirteen

GRACE FOR COWARDS

IT BEGAN WITH A CHANCE meeting on a night train speeding south from Paris to Vichy. A pretty French girl of 21, Jeannie Rousseau, met Georges Lamarque, only seven or eight years older but who had taught her at the University of Paris, where she had finished first in her class.

Jeannie spoke excellent German. She'd recently come to Paris from the coastal village of Dinard in Brittany, where she'd worked as a translator for the German command, and, unbeknown to the German officers or her father, passed on all the information she picked up to an underground agent.

Soon the British were receiving so much intelligence about German operations in the Dinard area that Nazi spies in London reported there must be a highly placed spy there. The gestapo arrested Jeannie in January 1941, and held her at the Rennes prison. But when an army tribunal tried her case, the officers from Dinard insisted that their charming translator couldn't possibly be a secret agent, and Jeannie was released. Her only punishment—an order to leave the coast.

So to Paris, where she looked for a new job that would give her access to truly sensitive information.

She found it on the Rue St. Augustin. She would translate for the French industrialists' syndicate. Soon she became the organization's top staff person, meeting regularly with the German military commander's staff to discuss commercial issues—inventories, strategic goods such as steel and rubber, and so on.

But she observed that certain offices and departments at the Hotel Majestic, where the German staff was based, were out of bounds. Behind those closed doors the Germans were working on special weapons and projects.

And then—the chance meeting on the night train to Vichy. Jeannie and Lamarque stood in the corridor, talking quietly under the dim light of a flickering light bulb. Slowly, guardedly Lamarque asked her what she was doing and then invited her to join an intelligence network known as the Druids that he was putting together. Her code name would be "Amniarix," and he would be her contact.

Neither could have dreamed what that conversation would lead to. Jeannie would eventually break one of the Nazis' most closely guarded secrets—the V-1 flying bombs and V-2 rockets that Hitler boasted would change the course of the war. At tremendous personal risk and in the face of harrowing hardship and suffering, a young girl would change the course of history. Only recently has her story come to light. She'd kept to herself the details of her heroic acts for more than half a century.

Jeannie had a brilliant mind and a photographic memory. She could absorb details of conversations with trusting German officers eager to impress the pretty young girl, who could have passed for a German and whom they all wanted to take to bed but who would never say yes, and so they desired her all the more because of it. Later she wrote out the conversations word for word, even when she didn't understand the technical details.

In a stroke of good fortune, Jeannie met several German officers who had been her friends at Dinard. They in turn introduced her to their friends—senior officers responsible for developing the secret weapons. These officers were a close-knit group that gathered evenings at a house to drink and talk and often invited Jeannie to join them. She listened and absorbed the details. Sometimes she teased and taunted, looking at them wide-eyed and saying they must be mad in speaking of an astounding new weapon that flew vast distances, and faster than any airplane. And to convince her the Germans brought out drawings and details of the test site at Peenenünde in Germany.

By September 1943 Jeannie had gathered information for a detailed report about the V-2 rockets. With a one-ton warhead, these new weapons would methodically destroy London and Britain's other large cities. Her precise information helped persuade Prime Minister Winston Churchill to bomb Peenemünde and thereby blunt the impact of Hitler's terror weapon.

In the spring of 1944 the British, impressed with Jeannie's work, decided to bring her to London for a debriefing. But the rescue operation was blown, and the gestapo captured her.

Now Jeannie found herself back in the same prison at Rennes, where she'd been detained in 1941. Her papers identified her as "Madeleine Chaufeur," and amazingly no one made the connection. The next 12 months were a struggle just to survive as she endured the horrors of three different concentration camps. Even during this nightmare she kept her wits about her. When transferred to the dreaded Ravensbruck, she reverted to her true name of Jeannie Rousseau, and her papers, sent separately under Madeleine Chaufeur, were never matched with her. The Nazis did not realize they were holding one of the key Allied spies.

Dying of tuberculosis and only days from death, Jeannie was saved near war's end by the International Red Cross. She weighed little more than 70 pounds.

How do you account for Jeannie Rousseau? Why did she risk her life when so many others were cowards?

"I just did it, that's all," she says. "It wasn't a choice. It was what you did. At the time, we all thought we would die. I don't understand the question. How could I not do it?"

Courage, said Winston Churchill, is the primary virtue

because it makes all other virtues possible. I think the old British bulldog was right.

I'm no hero, but I look back at scenes of my youth and wonder how I did it.

Turning 18, I was a shy, bookish university student more devoted to study than social activities. Two years earlier I'd been baptized and had become a member of the Seventh-day Adventist Church. Now, like other Ozzie boys my age, I was conscripted into "national service," the equivalent of the draft in America. But unlike most other young men, I didn't plan to carry a rifle in boot camp.

Australian law provided for conscientious objectors, but you had to persuade a magistrate personally about your convictions. The conference young people's leader accompanied me to the court, but I was the one who stood in the dock, swore on the Bible, and faced peppering from a state's attorney.

The magistrate granted my request, but the really hard part was still ahead. Each morning I lined up with the other soldiers and went through the drills—without a rifle. The platoon leader, Sergeant Gloyne, tried a series of ruses to get me to carry a gun, but I stood firm.

After a couple of weeks of drill, our platoon was ready for inspection. We spit-polished our boots, shined buckles, and pressed our uniforms. Then we marched to the parade ground, joined the other platoons, and went through the drills for the camp's commanding officer.

Talk about sticking out from the crowd—one young man without a gun on a parade ground with 1,000 soldiers! Before long the commanding officer summoned Sergeant Gloyne. I received the order "Fall out!" and was marched back to the barracks. That was the end of my army drills. For the remainder of boot camp I worked as a medical orderly or in the officers' mess hall.

Methinks grace is no feel-good, namby-pamby word. Grace supplies guts. Grace makes possible every other Christian quality.

In recounting this moment out of my life, I don't claim any superior virtue. That young person of 18 had a sincere aversion to bearing arms, and I still abhor killing and firearms. But I respect the convictions of people who don't share my views on this point—Christians who serve and fight to defend their country, law-enforcement officers, and others. I believe that God honors their consciences just as much as He honors mine.

But the point is that He *does* honor conscience. His grace gives us courage to do what seems impossible both in peace and war. Grace enables the spouse or daughter to care lovingly for the dear one afflicted with Alzheimer's disease. Grace sustains the harried mother of infants and little children. Grace helps us keep faithful to our vows and promises. Every day the stuff of life calls us to courage, and grace makes the weak—that's me—strong.

I have to share with you one of my favorite quotations. Because I have a thin skin, in many ways I'm ill-equipped to be an editor. That's why I keep Teddy Roosevelt's words pinned on the wall by my desk: "It is not the critic who counts, or the man who points out how the strong man stumbled, or where the doer of the deed could have done better. The credit belongs to the man who is actually in the arena; whose face is marred by dust and sweat and blood; who survives valiantly; who errs and comes short again and again; who knows great enthusiasms, great devotions, who spends himself in a worthy cause; who, at the best, knows in the end the triumph of high achievement; and who, at the worst, if he fails, at least fails while daring greatly, so that his place shall never be with those cold and timid souls who know neither victory nor defeat."

The Bible tells us that "the people that do know their God shall be strong, and do exploits" (Dan. 11:32). There's the secret of courage—in God, whose grace makes cowards like me capable of courageous living.

Chapter Fourteen

MY FAVORITE TEXT

TIME WAS I HAD A DECIDEDLY mixed reaction when people would say, "I'm praying for you." Although I'd try to thank them graciously, I was thinking: *Why do they say that? Do they think I'm not handling everything OK?*

No more. For many years now I've come to rejoice at the spoken or written messages of prayer support. They come frequently—some people uphold me and the staff daily—and every one is precious to me. I've felt myself and the entire ministry of the *Adventist Review* undergirded, upheld, even by the everlasting arms.

Gradually I have realized the truth of the seeming contradiction of the Christian life: When I am weak, then I am strong. And contrariwise: When I think I am strong, I am really weak and set up to fall flat on my face.

So one passage of Scripture took on new force in my experience until it became the ruling motif of my life: "To keep me from becoming conceited because of these surpassingly great revelations, there was given me a thorn in my flesh, a messenger of Satan, to torment me. Three times I pleaded with the Lord to take it away from me. But he said to me, 'My grace is sufficient for you, for my power is made perfect in weakness.' Therefore I will boast all the more gladly about my weaknesses, so that Christ's power may rest on me. That is why, for Christ's sake, I delight in weaknesses, in insults, in hardships, in persecutions, in difficulties. For when I am weak, then I am strong" (2 Cor. 12:7-10, NIV).

Here we catch the apostle Paul in an intimate moment. We don't know what his "thorn in the flesh" was—possibly a problem with his eyes, because the Galatians were ready to pluck out theirs to give to him (Gal. 4:15). Whatever, the affliction bothered Paul a great deal, and on three different occasions he labored with the Lord for deliverance.

But the Lord didn't give the answer that the apostle hoped for. That fact in itself provides an important insight about prayer. Because our request falls flat doesn't mean that we lack faith or that God turned a deaf ear. No! God may have a better answer in store for us, just as He had for Paul.

God didn't heal Paul, but He gave something much greater— grace. In spite of Paul's weakness, *because of* Paul's weakness, grace would be manifested that would be sufficient for every need. The problem would become the channel of a greater solution, the weakness a source of power that otherwise could not be manifested.

And the glory—for glory there would be—was all Christ's.

On numerous occasions and with increasing frequency, I've experienced the reality of these words. The Lord's promise to Paul has been fulfilled in my life and work. As my responsibilities increased over the years, I've had to travel extensively, often to destinations far away. On United Airlines alone I've logged more than a million miles. (Administrators in the General Conference travel much more; my experience isn't extraordinary in this environment.) Sometimes the trip involves concentrated speaking engagements, and worn out, I've wondered how I could ever find something coherent to say. But then I recalled this passage and claimed its promise. And the Lord always—always!—has come through with grace sufficient for the occasion.

The converse has shown itself starkly true also. Like other preachers, I've worked hard over a sermon, polished and prayed, delivered it, and sensed with the hearers the manifest presence of the Lord. And like other preachers, I've pulled out the same notes, spoken to a different audience, and felt a keen sense of disappointment at the lack of power.

When we think we are strong—when we see clearly how to proceed, have lined up our ducks, feel confident about the outcome—we really are weak. So often our work for the Lord is double-minded: We combine the Lord's power with our own resources, seeking to add His blessing and power to what we have planned and do. But when we are stripped naked, as it were, when we realize that we have nothing in ourselves—which in fact is always our condition—the contradiction of grace can sweep us up in its train.

Several years ago Noelene and I planned a trip to our native Australia. Because the Great South Land is still our home base, the church in its compassion provides us with the opportunity for periodic short visits to connect with our loved ones. Word of our coming got around, and the president of the Victorian Conference faxed to ask if I could arrive a few days early to speak at the camp meeting on Sabbath. Then the Western Australia Conference requested that I also try to fit in time with the elders of the conference, who would be gathering for several days of meeting. I looked at the calendar, figured out a way to put the appointments together, and said yes to both invitations.

I'd yet to learn that what may be possible isn't necessarily prudent.

I've made the trip to Oz many times, but it doesn't get easier. If you fly nonstop from Los Angeles or San Francisco, you're looking at 13-15 hours—depending on the strength of the winds—jammed into economy-class seats. Add on travel times across the United States, immigration checkpoints, and so on, and it's 30 or more hours from home to destination.

January's grip of cold and snow blanketed the East when I left America, and in Melbourne I ran into summer's height of heat and blinding light. The clock was 16 hours ahead of my body, and everything was turned around. At midnight I was wide awake; at midday I was fighting to stay awake.

My first appointment was the Friday night meeting, but I got a call earlier in the day. Would I mind meeting with the ministers and the church workers for an hour or so before "tea" ("supper" in American vernacular)? Again I said yes, spoke to the group, and prepared for the night meeting. Midway through my sermon the heavens, which had been darkening all day, opened up. A bolt of lightning struck the center pole of the big tent, sizzling the land-line carrying the meeting to the elderly residents' home nearby, and a deafening clap of thunder drowned out my voice. The lights and sound went off, sputtered, and eventually came back on.

On Sabbath I'd planned to preach twice, for the morning and evening services. But as I looked at the program I saw my name also listed for an afternoon meeting, 2:00–4:00 p.m.

"What's this?" I asked.

"Well, we figured you have stories of the church around the world that you'd like to share."

"OK. I presume you'll have a musical program, leaving me 30-40 minutes?"

"Well, not actually. We'd like you to take the whole time."

Which I did. And after a break I spoke for the evening program.

Sunday morning I had to leave for the airport to catch the plane to Perth across the continent. By now I was dead tired and hoping to find a few hours' rest in flight before I joined the elders for their discussions.

The meetings in Western Australia were being held in the church on the campground. As I arrived I bumped into Barry Oliver, who at that time taught at Avondale College.

"Hello, Bill," he said. "I'm just leaving. It's over to you now."

"What do you mean? Aren't there other presenters?"

"No. I've carried the program the past two days. Now you're it."

And I was.

Sunday night meeting. Several more presentations on Monday.

It was hot, and the church wasn't air-conditioned. By

Monday night and the final meeting I was dead on my feet, a zombie, my body crying out for sleep.

Somehow the Lord got me through the day and even the night. Somehow I was almost home free. And then . . .

Whenever I'm with a group for some time, I like to open up the floor for questions. I'd done so earlier in the day, and I did so for the last 30 minutes.

It was time to quit. The Lord had sustained me wonderfully. Time to sit down.

But I took one last question. From a man on the back row, who'd come in late and whose body language suggested he wasn't exactly a fan of mine. Beware of the last question—especially when it comes from a person on a back row who comes in late!

It was supposed to be a question, but it wasn't. It was a tirade, a blast. He lit into me and the *Review*, castigated me for what I'd done and hadn't done.

From my perspective his remarks were inaccurate, unfair, and uncharitable. But I was totally out of gas. Indeed, I'd been running on fumes all day. Now even the fumes were all spent.

I couldn't think. I could hardly stand. I just wanted to lie down and sleep.

Then I heard a voice speaking and with a shock realized that it was mine. "My friend," it said, in calm, even tones, "I don't know who you are and why you have said what you did. I don't agree with your opinion, but you have a right to it. I don't think these matters are appropriate to take up with the whole group, but if you care to see me privately after the meeting, I'll be glad to discuss them with you."

I sat down. Of course he didn't take me up on the invitation, and I went to bed and slept like a baby.

Never have I been at such a low point, so weak. I'd pushed myself to the limit and beyond; I'd been a foolish steward. But the Lord didn't forsake me in my extremity. Never have I experienced His taking over in such dramatic fashion.

Ellen White got it right: "Nothing is apparently more helpless, yet really more invincible, than the soul that feels its nothingness and relies wholly on the merits of the Saviour. By prayer, by the study of His Word, by faith in His abiding presence, the weakest of human beings may live in contact with the living Christ, and He will hold them by a hand that will never let go" (*The Ministry of Healing*, p. 182).

Our God promises to supply all our need according to His riches in Christ Jesus. And He does! His grace is all-sufficient. No matter what situation we face—stress, temptation, perplexity, heartbreak—His power will be made perfect in our weakness.

Ever asked yourself: What would be the worst situation that I would have to face? What would leave me feeling more desolate than anything else I could imagine?

I've thought about this and concluded that it would be the loss of the one whose life has been intertwined with mine for more than 40 years. To have to face each day without her, to have to walk alone—at this point the thought seems unbearable.

But even if that should happen, the promise will still be there, the promise of all-sufficient grace. Nothing—not death or life, not demons or men, not fear or failure—can cause it to fail. His grace will be there, always there, glowing and all-powerful in the midst of weakness.

Chapter Fifteen

AMADEUS

IN NOVEMBER 1783 A YOUNG couple, en route to their home in Vienna, stopped off at the Austrian town of Linz. Their host, Count Johann Thurn, was a lover of fine music and had an orchestra of his own of considerable merit. The 27-year-old husband was a musician and composer of some renown and thought he might repay the count's hospitality by performing one of his own compositions.

But when he searched through his bags he couldn't find anything he deemed suitable. He'd composed several symphonies, but they were all in Vienna. What to do?

He wrote a new one for the occasion. Working at breakneck speed, he completed the symphony in just four days. A full work that takes about 30 minutes to perform, Symphony No. 36 in C has passages of profound expression and is surely one of history's most valuable house presents. The next day, just the fifth after the couple's arrival, the count's orchestra played the piece.

Most composers take many months and often years to produce anything comparable to this piece, which has become popularly known as the "Linz Symphony." For any other composer we would probably call it great, but for this man we simply say it's good.

The 27-year-old was Wolfgang Amadeus Mozart, and his work redefined genius and greatness. So pure, so perfect were his finest compositions that the Linz, for all its qualities, has to take secondary rank.

Mozart sprang from a highly musical family. His father, Leopold, was a talented violinist in the employ of the archbishop of Salzburg, who exercised civil as well as spiritual authority over the pretty Austrian town and surrounding countryside. Leopold married Anna Maria Pertl, who bore him seven children. Only two survived infancy: Maria Anna, whom the family called Nannerl, and her brother younger by five years, Wolfgang Amadeus.

Nannerl was a bright, musical girl, but the young brother, even as a toddler, displayed amazing facility. Before he was 3 he began to pick out simple chords on the keyboard of the clavier. Soon he was composing little pieces of his own.

One evening when Wolfgang was 4, Leopold and a friend returned from church to find the little boy hard at work with pen and paper. Leopold asked, "What's that you're doing?"

"Writing a clavier concerto."

Leopold and his friend looked at the paper covered with inkblots and smears, and laughed. But as Leopold examined the notes more closely, his laughter died away. "Look at how correct and orderly it is," he said in amazement, "only it's so extraordinarily difficult, nobody in the world could play it."

"That's why it's a concerto; it has to be practiced," interrupted his young son. And going to the keyboard, he tried to demonstrate what he had in mind.

Soon Leopold realized he'd fathered a genius and decided to set his own career aside. He would expose his two gifted children to the world—the extraordinarily talented Nannerl and her incredible young brother.

Tour after tour followed in quick succession. Months away from home in the capitals of Europe. Performances for kings and emperors, popes and archbishops. The Mozart children became the talk of the continent.

Father and son visited Rome at Easter, 1770, just after Mozart's fourteenth birthday. They arrived in time to be present in the Sistine Chapel for the yearly performance of Allegri's *Miserere,* a complex choral work for four soloists and a five-part chorus. The Vatican, jealous of this musical treasure, allowed no copies to circulate, threatening the chapel musicians with excommunication if they leaked the score. But after one hearing Wolfgang nonchalantly wrote out the entire nine-part work from memory. When word of this got out, it caused a sensation. Pope Clement XIV conferred on the boy the Order of the Golden Spur.

Nannerl grew into her teens and lost her prodigy appeal. But the precocious boy continued to tour with his father and once with his mother (who died in Paris on the journey).

Amadeus did not expend himself as a comet that blazes brightly and then falls dark. As he grew, his talent blossomed into compositions that rank among the greatest of all time. His prodigious output—more than 600 works—is marvelous not for its size or even its variety, but for the number of times his works reached the summit of musical magnificence.

For all his genius Mozart's life was marked by increasing stress. His father saw in his gifted son the source of the entire family's financial security and endeavored to control him, for years nurturing the myth of Mozart as the eternal child. Eventually the son went his own way in a bitter split with his father and family that was never healed. Nor did Mozart ever find the wealthy patron who would supply him a place of relative comfort to compose at leisure. Taxed with the burdens of supporting a wife and growing family, he faced increasing financial pressures that he could relieve only by turning out more and more compositions.

Feverishly working on the *Requiem,* which a mysterious stranger had commissioned, he fell ill in mid-November 1791 and had to go to bed. A few minutes after midnight on December 5 it was all over. He was only 35.

A handful of friends gathered for his funeral. But the weather was bad, and no one accompanied his coffin to its final resting place. The person who was arguably the most musically gifted individual Western civilization has ever produced, whose works are performed and played more than any other composer in our day, was buried in a common, unmarked grave. To this day, no one knows its exact location.

I find it impossible to describe the music of this man. For years it has revived me, relaxed me, set my soul at rest, turned loose my own creative powers, limited as they are alongside his. Today books talk about "the Mozart effect"—how playing Mozart to babes and young children helps their minds develop, increases their intelligence, and so on. Studies with students allege that hearing his music increases problem-solving ability and examination scores. None of this surprises me. Amadeus has been doing it for me for 20 years.

An amazing thing about his music is that so much of it works for everybody. His melodies are so pure and so perfect that toddlers enjoy them along with adults. You hear the bars of "Tum, tetum, te ta ta tetum" of *Eine kleine Nachtmusik* start up anywhere in the world—from the jungles of Irian Jaya to the jungles of the Beltway—and you feel the music ironing the creases out of your brain.

As Mozart grew older and became ever more embroiled in a web of financial stress, pressures, and disappointment, his music became more complex, more shaded with dark amid the light. The young Mozart's work was unalloyed joy, however—music that sings, skips, laughs, jokes, and exults. And even in his last years, when works of greatness still sprang from his flying pen, passages of lyric lightness forced their way through the gathering somberness.

Let it be said loud and clear: This genius to whom I owe so much was no saint. His achievements came not as reward but as gift. That gift includes the early heavenly "Alleluia," only a few minutes long but transporting in its unutterable beauty and adoration, as well as a host of other compositions that lift the spirit at any hour of the day or night. That gift also includes operatic works of powerful music but trivial themes.

Amadeus sprang from a musical background, but his gift

exceeds anything that heredity can explain. Nothing can account for this gift—nothing.

Except grace.

Chapter Sixteen

LIVING IN GRACE

SO WONDERFUL IS THE LIFE lived in communion with Jesus—the life of grace—that no theological treatise or sermon can ever capture it. Jesus Himself didn't attempt to spell it out; He told stories.

One of my favorites is His parable of the shepherd and the flock (John 10:1-18). Here Jesus lays aside titles of royalty and power and calls Himself "the good shepherd." That in itself must have startled His hearers. Shepherds were low on the totem pole of first-century Judaism and were considered to be shifty fellows whose word couldn't be trusted in a court of law.

But at Messiah's birth God bypassed the strong and the mighty, the elite and the learned, and revealed the glad tidings to shepherds keeping watch over their flocks by night. And now, as Messiah's earthly career runs to its denouement, He likens Himself to a shepherd and His people to His flock.

"He calls his own sheep by name and leads them out," Jesus says (verse 3, NIV). Living in grace means that we know God loves us individually, knows our name, and has a tender regard for everything that happens to us.

Our name—how precious it is to us! In a crowd

with a thousand sounds we pick it out. I grew up in a family with plenty of Bills. When I came along my oldest sister, Gladys, whom everyone called Bonnie, was dating a man named Bill (whom she married in due course), and I was named after him. Later my youngest sister, Margaret, whom I have always known as Mollie, met and married another Bill. So at family gatherings there was old Bill, Bill, and young Bill or Billy.

To complicate matters even further, our daughter at one point dated a young man named—you guessed it—Bill. In the year the America's Cup was held in Perth, Western Australia, they decided to take a trip together to see Oz. Noelene and I also visited our homeland that year, so at one time there were four Bills all in the same room. When during the conversation someone mentioned "Bill," four heads snapped around in unison.

We remember those who know our name—they are special people to us. The best person at this—recalling names—has to be Neal C. Wilson, former General Conference president. He knows thousands of people by name and often can pull out of his mind names of their children, also. It's a marvelous gift he has, but one he has cultivated. Because he is interested in people, he tries to get their names down pat.

I well recall the first time I met Elder Wilson. Our family had come from India to Berrien Springs, Michigan, and I'd begun to teach at the seminary. I'd heard him speak in public, but we'd never met one-on-one. As I was walking across the broad, flat campus, I saw him at a distance coming toward me. I got ready to introduce myself, but he strode up to me, extending his hand as he greeted, "Hello, Bill. How are you?"

I was astounded. And impressed. Elder Wilson made me feel important. He valued me enough to know my name before we even met.

So does Jesus. He knew me before I knew Him. He called me by name, called me to Him. He values me and has a high and holy purpose for me, even though He knows my flaws and failings.

The Good Shepherd wants to lead me. I often think I know a

better way, often am slow to follow. But I look back on the course of my life and have a profound sense that the Good Shepherd has guided me all the way, at the crossroads of life and in a myriad of daily decisions.

"He calls his own sheep by name and leads them out," says Jesus (verse 3, NIV). "When he has brought out all his own, he goes on ahead of them, and his sheep follow him because they know his voice. But they will never follow a stranger; in fact, they will run away from him because they do not recognize a stranger's voice" (verses 4, 5, NIV).

Once I worked as a researcher in chemical technology. I had trained, earned my degree, was good at the work (the university gave me a gold medal at the end of the course), and even liked it. But one day I wrote a letter of resignation and left it on the desk of the chief chemist.

Why? Why turn my back on everything I had struggled to achieve? Why give up a career and launch out into the boundless deep?

The decision to leave chemistry and go to Avondale College to train for the ministry was the toughest one of my life. I wrestled with the Lord for months over it, arguing, reasoning, trying to convince Him and myself that it would be all wrong.

On my last day with the company I received a message that the CEO wanted to see me. I'd never met him, so I wondered what was going on as I opened his door and made my way across the big office to the chair at his desk.

"Well, Bill, I wanted to meet you," he said. "Your leaving has caused quite a stir—we thought you had a good future here. A lot of people think what you're doing is crazy, but I think I understand."

He got out of his chair and sat down next to me. "I am active in my church. In fact, I'm a lay preacher in the Presbyterian church. I can understand what is going through your mind.

"But listen: after you have spent a year at that school in the bush, you may be ready to come back to us. I want you to know that you'll have a place here."

The way he said it and the look in his eyes told me: You'll be back. As I walked across the expanse of carpet to the door, I could feel his eyes drilling holes in my back.

I never went back, never looked back. When after three years at Avondale the call came to uproot again and go to India, that decision was easy for me. The big one had paved the way.

The point is that Jesus knows best. He wants to lead us because He sees the future, has a perfect plan, and knows where we'll fit best. He'll never place us like a square peg in a round hole.

To me a life led by Christ is incredibly fulfilling. It's giving up nothing that really matters to gain everything. With the psalmist I can sing: "You have made known to me the path of life; you will fill me with joy in your presence, with eternal pleasures at your right hand" (Ps. 16:11, NIV). So rich and satisfying has my life been that if it should end today I would die the happiest of men.

Ellen White wrote a passage along these lines that has meant much to Noelene and me. It comforted us as we dealt with the call to India, and we've come back to it time and time again. "Those who decide to do nothing in any line that will displease God will know, after presenting their case before Him, just what course to pursue. And they will receive not only wisdom, but strength" (*The Desire of Ages*, p. 668).

We will *know!* She does not tell us how we will know. God has a multitude of ways of revealing His will to us. His counsel may come as a conviction that forms deep within us, as a sudden awareness as we walk, as the word of a friend, or as an insight from the Scriptures that speaks to our situation. But we will know.

To someone reading this who doesn't recognize Jesus as the Good Shepherd, these words must seem strange. I hope they sound inviting, because to those of us who know Him they are the very stuff of life. The life of grace is life in a new dimension, life with a high that never leaves you with a hangover.

For many years now I've been editor in chief of the *Adventist Review*. The task is unrelenting: We go to press every week of the year without fail. Our staff is small for the responsibilities we carry, and the possibilities of a major boo-boo are high—something that would be an embarrassment to us and to the church and would let down our Lord. And print is unforgiving. Even though you may run a correction or apology in the following issue, you can never undo what has gone out to the four winds.

Only by the daily grace of our gracious Lord can we do this work. Only His daily grace protects us from ourselves.

I cannot begin to list the numerous occasions when His leading has spared us from major blunders, sometimes at the eleventh hour—when we've pulled material just before press time; when we "just happened" to find an article of the right content and length to replace it; when we changed our minds about hiring a new staff member after a long search had pointed in a certain direction.

No matter what our situation in life may be, we all carry a load of cares. Jesus offers us a life, not without cares, but without the added burden of worrying about them. He tries to tell us that He loves us so much, loves us individually, that He will go on ahead of us. He'll lead us through this life and to our eternal home with Him.

But the life of grace is even more. Listen to another of my favorite texts: "Those who hope in the Lord will renew their strength. They will soar on wings like eagles; they will run and not grow weary, they will walk and not be faint" (Isa. 40:31, NIV).

A few years ago I was asked to preach at a combined meeting of several Adventist churches in central Ohio. One week before, in the early hours of a Sunday morning in Paris, the princess of Wales breathed her last after an auto accident. The beautiful, shy rich girl who had everything and yet nothing was gone, and the world was hurting.

Before we gathered for worship that morning, Diana's body had been carried to Westminster Abbey for a moving service of music, remembrances, and last respects. Vast crowds had lined the streets of London, weeping as the bier passed by, followed by the two motherless sons on foot.

Diana was on everybody's hearts and minds that day, and I

got up early and reworked the sermon to talk about her beautiful, sad, tragic life. The church was packed, and the people, many of whom had risen to watch the funeral on television, listened attentively. Behind me was the best supporting cast I've ever had in my public work—the choir from nearby Mount Vernon Academy. Already they'd provided wonderful choral music. Now they entered into the sermon with an enthusiasm that I could hear and feel.

I closed with the words of Isaiah 40:31 and felt an even greater burst of energy from the young people behind me. The choir director could hardly wait to tell me afterward that this text was their motto, and she presented me with a T-shirt that I treasure to this day. It's made of simple white cloth with the outline of a flying eagle and the words of the text. However, "hope," "renew," and "soar" are printed in large red letters so that they jump out from the rest.

The T-shirt has developed a life of its own.

I wore it as I was out walking in San Diego. As a man passed me he turned around and caught up with me. "Do you mind?" he asked. "What are those words on your T-shirt?"

I showed him, told him how I'd gotten it. We kept talking, got onto India, and his eyes lighted up—his grandfather was a longtime missionary to that country.

Wearing the T-shirt, I walk to the local supermarket. I wonder why the people in the adjacent checkout line are looking hard at me until I realize they're trying to read the words.

It was the last Sunday in October and time for my annual flirtation with elation and desperation—the Marine Corps Marathon. Temperatures at this time of the year are supposed to be in the 50s or 60s, but this particular day was going to be hot. Before the race ended, hundreds would be treated by paramedics and some 4,000 of the 18,000 starters would drop out.

For tortoises like me, the run presented two challenges: first, to get across the Fourteenth Street Bridge before 2:00, when the marines reopen the road to traffic and bus stragglers to the finish line. And second, to somehow complete the last four miles beyond the bridge to the 26.2-mile point, where the marines will congratulate you, put the medallion around your neck, and wrap a blanket over your shoulders.

I was wearing the Isaiah 40:31 T-shirt. My runner's number covered up most of the text, leaving "hope" to stand out even more. As I plodded through the streets of Georgetown, the crowds shouted, "Go, Hope!" Past the Capitol. Down Constitution Avenue. Past the Washington Monument. On to the Lincoln Memorial. Then the long grind toward Hains Point and the 19-mile mark. This stretch is where many give up, where every year I figure this is the craziest thing I've ever done in my life and vow never to try it again.

The clock was running, and it was getting hotter and hotter. The marines were running out of water—a cruel blow as I staggered up to the aid stations. By 1:40 I'd come up the slope leading to the bridge. Everyone left in the race was walking now, breaking into slow runs occasionally. The sun beat down mercilessly on the bridge, and we faced into its full glare. All along the road the runners were laid out, with paramedics bending over them; ambulances shuttled back and forth.

But the T-shirt still shouted "Hope!" Underneath the number it said "Renew!" And also "Soar," but I was happy just to walk, just to keep on going, just to get across the bridge.

And then, the long bridge behind, new life surged back. I could do it. I would finish this race. I would cross that finish line. I might even enter again the next year.

Chapter Seventeen

FIGHTING GRACE

EVER FEEL THAT THE WORLD has gone so far to the dogs that you can't see how it could get any worse? That, as Billy Graham once said, if Jesus doesn't come back soon He'll have to apologize to Sodom and Gomorrah?

Recently I heard about school days in the 1950s. The biggest problems high school teachers faced were—guess what? Chewing gum, spit wads, and revving cars in the parking lot!

I think of what's happening today, of the mayhem at midday in Littleton, Colorado, when two high school seniors went berserk, killing 12 of their fellows, a beloved teacher, and finally themselves. Shock waves from the massacre reverberated around America and the world. Although America and some other countries have suffered school shootings in recent years, this one made the blood run cold. Here were two boys who planned and prepared for a year to kill as many people as possible, who assembled an arsenal of weapons and bombs, and who giggled and laughed as they shot at point-blank range.

Then I think of the 1950s—spit wads? Whatever happened to us in just 40 years? Will this horrendous situation ever turn around? How can it go any lower when already it's the pits?

No wonder that as we come to a new millennium so many thinking people are pessimistic. A world-renowned figure like Jacques Cousteau went to his grave forecasting doom for the human race because our insatiable greed and wanton abuse of the planet's resources are driving us to mass suicide. Others predict that a rogue asteroid will slam into Earth with a force that will blanket the globe in dust, giving us a year-round winter that will destroy crops and cause us to starve. No wonder movies such as *Armageddon* fill the box offices, and *Titanic* makes the biggest hit of all time.

Evil seems everywhere pervasive. Every new invention, every advance in technology, becomes a tool for new manifestations of wickedness. Once men and women bought porn magazines and carried them home in brown-paper wrappings, ashamed to be seen looking at them. Today the Internet makes available the vilest material imaginable in the secrecy of one's own home. That same Internet has become an instrument used by pedophiles and other perverts to lure and trap children.

I sometimes tremble at the odds stacked against young people today. How can young men and women act with integrity when all around them their peers—by their own admission—are lying and cheating? How can young persons stay pure when the media through images and sounds glorify promiscuity and mock virginity and when—even worse—their own parents are jumping in and out of bed with other partners?

We've reached a stage in history when evil rages unchecked. We feel numb as we learn of outrageous deeds—deeds we couldn't imagine. A teenage girl gives birth to a child, suffocates it, throws it in a trash can, cleans herself up—and returns to the dance floor! The very young, the very old, clerics, nuns—no one is immune from assault and murder. Nothing is off-limits anymore; nothing is so vile, so sordid that it cannot be written about or viewed. Isn't this humanity's last gasp?

By the time you read this far, I can hear you saying, "Bill must be having a really bad day. I thought he was an optimist."

I am. All that I described above—and I could go on and write a book detailing the reign of evil in our society, except that I choose not to wallow in filth—would weigh me down except for one thing. You guessed it—grace!

I want to tell you this, and I want you to get it because I hang my life on it: *As powerful a force as evil is in our world, grace is even more powerful.*

Grace is no namby-pamby word, no feel-good catchcry. Grace has a strong, tough aspect that will surprise you. Grace is militant; grace fights.

Now you're pushing it, you say. Fighting grace? Where do you find that in the Bible?

Right at the beginning, in the very first promise of Scripture. Here's the picture: Our first parents fell because they believed the devil rather than God. They'd forfeited their right to life and God's presence; they were now slaves to the evil one. But God gave them hope. Addressing the serpent, He said: "And I will put enmity between you and the woman, and between your offspring and hers; he will crush your head, and you will strike his heel" (Gen. 3:15, NIV).

Note that word "enmity." It means "hatred," and we usually don't associate it with the Christian life. But here it's a word that rings with hope and deliverance.

Remember, God was speaking to that ancient enemy, Satan. He made a fantastic prophecy: One descendant of the woman, Eve, would crush the serpent's head. Yes, the serpent would hurt that "seed" (singular)—he will bruise the heel. And so, in the fullness of God's time, a Child was born, a descendant of Eve after hundreds of generations. No ordinary baby boy this: He was Emmanuel, God with us, God Himself taking our flesh and coming to live among us.

And to die! After a life of gentle and noble deeds, a life given wholly to healing and helping others, He was cut off at 30, pinned to a Roman cross just outside the city of Jerusalem.

The ancient enemy exulted that day. He'd dogged Jesus' footsteps all along the way. He'd tried to get Him killed as a babe; he'd tempted Him to short-circuit His saving mission in the wilderness;

he'd tried to make Him turn back as the woes of the human race pressed upon Him in the garden; he'd taunted Him as He hung upon Calvary. And he saw Him expire, saw Him laid in Joseph's rock-cut tomb.

But the serpent only bruised Jesus' heel. On Sunday morning before first light He rose from the dead, burst its bands, and went forth a mighty conqueror, Lord of heaven and earth, Lord of life and the grave. Praise God for our mighty Deliverer!

One day, however, the other half of the prophecy will reach fulfillment. One day the ancient enemy will receive his due. One day he who has brought death to so many will himself die under God's hand as the serpent's head is crushed forever. The book of Hebrews tells us: "Since the children have flesh and blood, he [Jesus] too shared in their humanity so that by his death he might destroy him who holds the power of death—that is, the devil—and free those who all their lives were held in slavery by their fear of death" (Heb. 2:14, 15, NIV).

These words assure us that one day evil will be no more. No more pain and suffering, crime and destruction, war and weapons, refugees and starving children, lust and greed, violence and rape, filth and lies. All these things will pass away, along with their father, the devil.

But what about the meantime? How do we get from here to there, from now to then? How can the flood of evil ever be dammed up?

Genesis 3:15 tells us how, with that little, wonderful word "enmity." God promised to put hatred between the woman and her descendants (that's us) and the serpent. We don't put it there, because we cannot. We're bent toward evil. We're born that way. "As the twig is bent, the tree will grow." It's easier for us to lie than to tell the truth, to lust than to love, to follow the devil than to hate him.

But God does what we cannot. He puts within us a divine capacity to do what doesn't come naturally, to follow Him rather than the serpent.

That divine capacity, that hatred, that enmity, is grace.

Grace fights. Grace enables us to do what is humanly impossible. Grace changes us from children of evil to children of righteousness.

Grace fights, and grace wins. Grace is stronger than evil.

Without grace, the whole world would lie like pawns in evil's hand. Without grace, not one person would honor God. Without grace, every vestige of beauty, truth, and nobility would vanish.

Without grace, you wouldn't be reading this book, and I wouldn't have written it.

Notice how my favorite Christian writer puts it: "It is the grace that Christ implants in the soul which creates in man enmity against Satan. Without this converting grace and renewing power, man would continue the captive of Satan, a servant ever ready to do his bidding. But the new principle in the soul creates conflict where hitherto had been peace. The power which Christ imparts enables man to resist the tyrant and usurper. Whoever is seen to abhor sin instead of loving it, whoever resists and conquers those passions that have held sway within, displays the operation of a principle wholly from above" *(The Great Controversy*, p. 506).

The writer, Ellen White, titled her book *The Great Controversy Between Christ and Satan.* That title is accurate, but the conflict rages far wider. Not just Christ and Satan, but people—we—are part of the struggle. Because of the enmity-fighting grace, we have a choice. We can cast our vote and our life on one side or the other.

So, no matter how dark the night, it is never without stars. For every atrocity there's an act of heroism; for every act of cowardice, a deed of bravery. Fighting grace takes possession of men and women, and they refuse to let evil roll on unchecked. They stand up and fight back. A William Wilberforce rises up to expose the slave trade and fight it to the death. A Florence Nightingale goes to the Crimea to minister to the wounded and dying. A Rosa Parks refuses to sit in the back of the bus.

Slowly, slowly, against terrible odds, the clouds of exploitation and injustice and racism roll back. Grace fights, and grace wins.

The most deep-seated pride of the human heart, I believe, is that of our ethnic identity. This pride is a two-edged sword that cuts with terrible force for good or ill. It cuts one way and gives us a healthy sense of who we are; it gives us dignity and self-respect. But it cuts the other way and leads us to dehumanize or even demonize those whose origins differ from ours. When we no longer regard persons of a particular ethnic group as truly human, we feel free to kill and maim them without reason and without mercy.

That's what happened in Rwanda. Peoples who had lived harmoniously side by side for several generations turned on one another in mass destruction. For the majority it made no difference that they were professedly Christians. The evil of ethnic hatred exploded and made the land a bloodbath.

But grace is greater than the evil of ethnic hatred. The killing will not stop because the Tutsis wipe out the Hutus, or the Hutus the Tutsis. The killing will stop only as grace in its quiet power leavens enough human hearts.

Listen to this true story, which I share just as it was first published.*

"She got into our van as we headed for an orphanage in a nearby town. The bus would take forever, and Carl Wilkens and I were going her direction, so it was no problem to take another passenger. As we bumped over the potholed road, I noticed a deep scar across her forehead and another on the back of her head. Carl noticed too, and being curious, he asked her about them. She spoke in her native language, with a local pastor interpreting her story into English, as we drove past the deceptively green hills of Rwanda.

"During the recent political upheaval in which thousands of people were killed, a man attacked her, she said. The man killed her pastor-husband and left her for dead, with machete slashes across her face and head. But when all was safe, her son came from his hiding place and rescued her, saving her life.

"But the story she told only began there. She spoke with emotion as she continued. 'During the terrible slayings I saw the man who killed my husband and wounded me. I had known him well. He had once been a member of my husband's congregation. Of course, the man did not know that I was not dead when he walked away.'

"Then months later, while shopping in a busy, crowded outdoor marketplace, she came face-to-face with him. They each stood still, staring at each other for a moment, unable to move. The man was shocked to see her alive—this pastor's wife whom he was sure he'd killed in the fury of the massacre. He never expected to see her face again. Would her husband also appear before him now?

"He began to sweat profusely, thinking he was seeing a ghost. But she did not disappear—she just stood there in the market, looking back at him, her scars deep from his own machete.

"The horror of it all rushed over him. He trembled at what her response would be to him now. Would she turn him over to the police to be tried for his crime? He had seen that happen so often since the terrible killings had ended, and many were now in prison for their part in the slayings.

"His eyes seemed glued to her expression of recognition. He was unable to run. There was no escape. Other people in the market became aware of the confrontation and watched to see what would happen as perspiration continued to roll down the criminal's face and chest. He knew he'd been caught.

"The crowd began to ask, 'Why is he acting like this? What is wrong with this man?'

"Turning to them, the pastor's wife said calmly: 'This man saw me in the hospital when I was very sick, and he did not think I was going to live. That is why he is so surprised to see me today.'

"Then she walked up to the man and spoke his name, saying, 'Come with me.'

"She took him to her home and exchanged his sweat-drenched shirt for a clean one from her own son's closet. Then she said words that must have been the hardest words that she'd ever spoken: 'I don't know what else you have done or who else might accuse you, but as for me, I forgive you.'

"And the man went his way. She doesn't know where he went. But she now goes from house to house selling books as a literature evangelist, telling others of God's love and forgiveness.

"As Carl and I took the woman to her small house in the nearby town, I knew something inside me had changed. Her story of the ultimate forgiveness would remain with me forever. I still see her scars when I close my eyes really tight."

I believe grace is constantly fighting the good fight, constantly working to roll back the darkness and bring hope and new life.

Police officer Kelly Benitez was driving around in his cruiser in Los Angeles. He noticed a car with expired registration tags and pulled it over. He approached the driver and asked to see his license. Benitez stared at it for a long time—Paul Benitez!

"What do you know?" he said. "You and I have the same name."

The older man behind the wheel looked hard at him and then exclaimed, "You're my son!"

Yes, it was his son whom he'd last seen when Kelly was only 4 months old and the parents separated. Police officer and offender, son and father, experienced a strange, joyful reunion.

What are the odds of this encounter happening in a city the size of Los Angeles? Coincidence—or just one more glimpse of grace?

And by the way, the father didn't get a ticket that day.

I was in Iguaçu at the southern end of Brazil for a church council, and Mack Tennyson called me over. Mack teaches accounting at the University of Charleston in South Carolina, and we've had interesting conversations in the past. That day his face was beaming, and he was bursting to tell me something.

It was about his little girl—his new little girl.

A year earlier he and his wife, Sharon, had made arrangements to adopt a child in China. Without seeing her they decided to name her Alexandra Mae after Mack's maternal grandmother.

My blood ran cold as Mack described their visit to the orphanage where they were to pick up their child. Mack and Sharon saw 50 1-year-old children lying in little beds. None of them had been held close by adults; all were kept tied down. The staff of the orphanage didn't have the time to give the children individual care, so they kept them secure in bed.

They took Alexandra Mae and held her close. She could not

hold her head up straight, let alone sit, crawl, or walk. Her normal development had been arrested as she lay day after day tied down in bed.

As Mack carried her from the orphanage, he looked back and saw the long rows with little faces looking up from where they lay. One bed was now empty.

Mack and Sharon usually don't choose five-star accommodations when they travel, but this time Mack had asked for the best hotel in town in order to minimize health risks. He carried little Alexandra up to their room and laid her between the fresh white sheets. As he saw her lying there, one child out of the 50 plucked out and given a chance for love and life, it struck him—grace! Alexandra had done nothing to deserve it; she didn't have any natural beauty to distinguish her from the others; she'd simply been picked up and set free.

At that moment Mack himself had an overwhelming sense of being blessed, that this was a special child given him by God. He decided that her name wouldn't be Alexandra Mae but Alexandra Grace.

They brought the baby back to the United States and began to watch a miracle unfold. Alexandra Grace developed like a butterfly emerging from its chrysalis. All the stages arrested from her first year of life came marching by at fast-forward speed: She soon could hold her head straight, then sit up, then crawl, then walk.

Grace set her free to be all that God made her to be.

Early on, however, Sharon and Mack noticed that Alexandra seemed to look straight past them instead of focusing on them. When they placed her down on the rug she didn't pick out little bits of fiber as other babies do. They took her to a doctor, who held her close and pronounced, "This child can't see!" He fitted her with thick lenses, and immediately she began to focus.

Mack proudly showed me pictures of his girl, who was then 2 years old. She was about the cutest, happiest-looking miss you could find anywhere.

"She wears her glasses all day, right up to bed," said Mack.

"Then she'll give a big yawn, take them off, rub her eyes, and hurl the glasses at full force. Sharon and I have learned to be ready to make a dive for them—after all, they cost $400 to replace!"

Just one reminder, one scar from the past, remains. Like the other babies tied to their beds, for her first year Alexandra Grace had only one "toy" to play with—the end of the string tying her down. She still likes to suck on her bib string in her bed as she falls asleep.

Yes, friend of mine, I'm still an optimist. I'm not naive, not blind to the surge of evil that threatens to engulf society. But I think of Alexandra Grace Tennyson, of Kelly and Paul Benitez, of the nameless widow in Rwanda—and I take courage.

Evil is strong, but grace is stronger.

---

*Eric Guttschuss as told to Heather Guttschuss, "Left to Die," *Adventist Review*, Jan. 8, 1998.